52 TIPS
FOR NO-LIMIT
HOLD'EM POKER

BARRY SHULMAN
with Roy Rounder

Cardoza Publishing is the foremost gaming publisher in the world with a library of more than 200 up-to-date and easy-to-read books and strategies. These authoritative works are written by the top experts in their fields and with more than 10,000,000 books in print, represent the most popular gaming books anywhere.

Originally published by Card Player Press
Copyright © 2006, 2012 by Barry Shulman
- All Rights Reserved -

Library of Congress Catalog Card No: 2012933917
ISBN 10:   1-58042-310-8
ISBN 13: 978-1-58042-310-6

Visit our website or write for a full list of Cardoza Publishing books and advanced strategies.

CARDOZA PUBLISHING

P.O. Box 98115, Las Vegas, NV 89193
Toll-Free Phone (800)577-WINS
email: cardozabooks@aol.com
www.cardozabooks.com

About the Author

Barry Shulman, the 2009 World Series of Poker Main Event champion in Europe—he defeated Daniel Negreanu heads-up for the title—is a winner of more than $4.5 million in live tournament earnings. A two-time gold bracelet winner at the WSOP and winner of millions more at cash tables, he is one of the most accomplished Texas hold'em tournament players today.

Barry is also one of the most powerful and influential figures in the poker world. He is the chairman of Card Player Media, publisher of *Card Player*, the oldest-running and biggest poker magazine (more than 500,000 circulation monthly), with franchises around the world. He is the author of two terrific books, *52 Tips for Limit Hold'em Poker* and *52 Tips for No-Limit Hold'em Poker*.

Barry has expanded his online presence with several websites. **CardPlayer.com** is the largest and most informative poker portal in the world, while **CardPlayerPokerSchool.com** is one of the best free poker-training sites. Read more about Barry at **BarryShulman.com**, and follow his travel adventures at **JetSetWay.com**.

Acknowledgments

52 Tips is a series of concise how-to poker books that provide you with concise and easy-to-understand tips on how to become a winning poker player. Whereas the first *52 Tips* book dealt exclusively with limit hold'em, this book expands into the realm of the hyperpopular no-limit hold'em. Picking up where *52 Tips for Limit Hold'em Poker* left off, this new *52 Tips* focuses on the nuances that differentiate limit from no-limit hold'em.

I worked closely with professional poker player and author Roy Rounder on this book. Roy, who is primarily known for his award-winning newsletter, helped me verbalize the complex strategies of no-limit hold'em with a down-to-earth writing style. You can visit Roy at www.FreePokerNewsletter.com.

As was the case with the first *52 Tips*, Michael Wiesenberg edited the original book, putting the tips into clear and proper English. Additionally, he also expanded on the already extensive glossary. Thanks also goes to Bethany Scoggins, who worked diligently on the design and the layout of the entire book. Christy Devine did the cover photos and orchestrated the original look of the front and back cover designs.Dominik Karelus, who created and heads our Card Player Press division, was instrumental in publishing the first edition of this book.

Finally, I want to acknowledge and thank my son Jeff, who not only is my constant sounding board, but oversees everything at Card Player Media, including this project.

CONTENTS

Introduction

We're going to show you how to consistently win money at no-limit hold'em.

We have collected together the 52 most important and money-making concepts and strategies for no-limit Texas hold'em cash games and tournaments. While these tips are easy-to read and in bite-sized pieces, don't get fooled—the advice is very powerful. In fact, I used the very same strategies to win the World Series of Poker main event in Europe in 2009.

You will learn the most profitable way to bet in all key situations on all streets—preflop. flop, turn and river—and how to play draws, trouble hands, suited connectors, A-K and A-Q, middle pairs, premium pairs, and suited aces. You'll also learn how to attack and get chips from the various types of opponents you will encounter at the table—tight, loose, passive, and aggressive (and the various combinations of each)—while showing how to optimally adjust your play to the blinds, and to their stack size and yours.

No-limit hold'em is primarily situational, concerned more about what the other guy has and who he is than about your own hand. We will go over all of the key concepts so that every time you sit down to play no-limit hold'em, you'll bring a full arsenal of winning strategies to the table.

Here are 52 tips that will improve your no-limit hold'em game. Enjoy and be a winner!

How to Play No-Limit Hold'em

This section is for those who have not played hold'em before. It describes how to play a hand.

The Deal

Years ago players in all games dealt for themselves. The deal rotated clockwise (one position to the left) after each hand. Nowadays, most cardrooms have house dealers who deal all the cards, maintain table decorum, ensure the pots and betting are correct, see that players act in turn, and award pots to the winning players. The position from which the dealer would distribute cards if the dealer were one of the players is indicated by a **dealer button.** Most players call it simply the **button.** The button is often a white disk approximately the size of a hockey puck, sometimes labeled "button." From now on, when we speak of the button, we will be referring either to that disk or to the player who sits in that position. You'll be able to tell by context what we mean.

When the house dealer distributes cards to the players, he always starts with the player in the seat to the left of the button and ends with the button. All online cardrooms use a button, and it is a graphical representation of the preceding.

Antes and Blinds

Also in those old days, back when the main game in cardrooms was five-card draw, players put *antes* into each pot. An **ante** is a payment made by each player to the pot prior to receiving cards. An ante is not a bet because it does not "play for" the player. The purpose of the antes is to stimulate action. Without money in the pot, the first player would never have an incentive to open the betting because there would be nothing to win.

Antes are still used in forms of seven-card stud and they also appear in no-limit hold'em tournaments. Generally, though, hold'em-type games use *blinds*, which serve the same purpose as antes—to stimulate action. Unlike an ante, however, a **blind**, which is a forced wager, is considered to be a *bet* made before the cards are dealt, and it plays for the player. That is, an amount equal to the size of the blind is part of a player's bet later on.

Usually, the player to the immediate left of the button puts chips into the pot equal to half the size of the minimum bet for the game. Those chips (and the player who puts the chips in) are called the **small blind.** The next player to his left, that is, the player two positions to the left of the button, puts chips into the pot equal in size to the limit of the game. Those chips (and the player who puts the chips in) are called the **big blind.** For example, in a $5/$10 no-limit game, the small blind is $5 and the big blind is $10.

First Round

The dealer distributes one card face down to each player, starting with the small blind, and then another card. The cards are always dealt clockwise in any poker game. When each player has two **hole cards,** as they are called, the deal stops and the *action* begins. Here, **action** means betting, raising, and folding.

Hold'em has four rounds of betting

On the first round of betting, the action commences with the player immediately to the left of the big blind. Just as in the rotation of the deal and the distribution of cards, the action in any poker game always proceeds clockwise. The first player has three options. Let's use the $5/$10 game as our example. He can **fold** his hand (choose not to play and relinquish his cards to the dealer), **call** $10 (match the big blind, which is considered a bet, albeit one made without the player having seen his cards), or **raise** (increase the bet) by putting at least $20 into the pot.

In no-limit hold'em, there are virtually no limits on the amount a player can bet or raise. The only restriction is the size of a player's chip stack. This is the primary difference between no-limit hold'em and limit hold'em. In addition, there is no cap on the number of raises and reraises that can occur in each. In a limit game, a **cap** is the maximum number of bets allowed in a round, usually one bet plus three raises. In a no-limit game, there can be any number of raises, although usually a bet plus three or four raises is sufficient to exhaust any player's stack, because each raise generally becomes large compared to the sizes of the players' stacks.

When someone calls the big blind on the first betting round without raising, that is, by just betting or calling the minimum for the game, that is called **limping**.

Betting by the Blinds

On the first round of betting, the blinds act after everyone else. After the button has folded, called, or raised, the small blind acts. Since the small blind already has chips in the pot, if he plays he adds only as much to the pot as needed to make the total equal the bet. In our example of the $5/$10 game, we saw that the small blind has $5 that plays for him in the pot. If players have limped and there have been no raises, he can participate by adding $5 to the pot. Just as any other player, the small blind can fold, call, or raise. If anyone has raised before the action gets to the small blind, he would have to call the raise, less $5, to participate. For example, if a player raised to $20, the small blind can play by adding $15 to the pot.

The big blind is the last to act on the first round of betting. If one or more players have called the initial bet—that is, if the players have all limped—the big blind has two choices. This situation is called the **option**. He can elect to simply **check**—make no bet but retain his cards. This effectively ends the betting for the round. However, the big blind has another choice when the action gets to him with no raises. Even though he has already technically made a bet—the big blind, after all, is a bet—and there has been no raise, he can himself raise. In a **brick-and-mortar cardroom**—a cardroom having a real physical location, with live players, as opposed to an *online cardroom*—when the action gets to the big blind without anyone having raised, the house dealer usually says something like "Your option" or "Option." Sometimes the dealer just points at the player. In an online cardroom, when the action similarly gets to the big blind, the software presents two choices, one prompting "raise" and the other "check." The effect is the same.

If, however, there has been a raise, the big blind now must either match the raise (call), raise the pot himself, or fold his hand.

The Flop

After the action is complete for the first round, that is, at the point that all the betting has been equalized, the dealer places three cards face up in the center of the table. This is called the **flop**. These cards are called **community cards**, and each player uses them in combination with his own two cards. Each player tries to form the best five-card hand from some combination of his two hole cards and the five community cards that will eventually be dealt.

Because community cards are part of every player's hand, a flop of A-A-A is ordinarily nothing to get too excited about. Yes, you have three aces, but so do all your opponents. If you have the remaining ace in your hand, however, inner rejoicing may be appropriate.

A second round of betting now begins. This time the betting starts with the first *active player* to the dealer's left. (An **active player** is one who has met all the betting thus far.) The first round of betting is the only one in which the betting does not start immediately to the left of the button—and that is because of the blinds. The first player has two options. He can check or bet. Only in the first round must each player in turn bet or fold—also because of the blinds. If someone bets on the second round, each remaining player has three options: fold, call, or raise.

Once again, in no-limit hold'em there is no limit to the amount a player can bet or how many raises and reraises can occur in the round.

The Turn

The dealer places a fourth card faceup in the center of the table, adjacent to the three flop cards. This card is called the **turn**. Another round of betting follows and the players have the same betting options as the previous round. They can check or bet if no bet has yet been made, or they can fold, call, or raise if a bet has been made.

The River

Finally, the dealer places the fifth card faceup in the center of the table, adjacent to the four community cards already there. This card is known as the **river**. A final round of betting takes place, again with the same conditions.

When the betting has been equalized, there is a *showdown* of all remaining hands, and the best hand wins the pot. The **showdown** is the point at the end of the hand in which the cards are turned faceup and the best hand claims the pot.

If only one player remains; that is, there has been a bet or raise that has not been called, then that player wins the pot and no cards are shown. The exception is if any player has run out of chips, there still is a showdown, even though the betting has not been equalized. You can never be bet out of a pot just because you run out of chips before a hand is over. If you run out of chips and other players have chips left with which to bet, then a **side pot** is created that the all-in player cannot win. On the showdown, the best hand in contention for the main pot wins it, and the best hand in contention for the side pot wins that. The same hand might win both the main pot and side pot.

Reading the Board

If you are new to hold'em, one of your top priorities should be to learn how to accurately **read the board**, that is, how the community cards relate to your two cards. Reading the board in hold'em is not nearly as complex as in games such as Omaha eight-or-better. It's important, nonetheless.

These examples show situations that beginners sometimes misread.

Example 1

Your hand is the ace-high (**nut***) flush, which beats your opponent's hand. He uses his 7♥ with the 8♥ 9♥ 10♥ J♣ on the board to make a straight. If either the 6♥ or J♥ had been the river card, instead of the K♠, your opponent would have a straight flush. When you start with considerably the best of it, such as this situation of flopping the nut flush, and end up losing on the river to a straight flush against a player who starts with only one card of that suit, you have suffered what players call a **bad beat**. Part of the ability to read the board should include realizing that even if you have the nut flush, if three—or four!—cards to a straight flush are on the board, you might end up losing. And it will be costly if you do. So if a **solid opponent** (conservative, not likely to get out of line) raises on the turn or the river in a situation in which you think you have the nuts, take another look at the board to see if a better hand is possible.

Example 2

Who wins this hand? Although you have two pair, you lose the pot to your opponent's A-K. Why? He can play sevens and fours with an ace kicker, while you must **play the board**. That is, the best hand

---

*   **Nut** refers to the best possible hand for the situation. Thus a **nut flush** is the best possible flush that can be made. With four hearts on the board, for example, whoever holds the A♥ has the nut flush. Similarly, with a board of 6♥ 7♦ 8♦ Q♥ A♣, anyone with holecards 9-10 of any suits would have the nut straight. That hand would also be known as the nuts, because it is the best possible hand that can be made with that board.

you can make by using the best five of the seven available to you is what's on the board, sevens and fours with a 5 kicker. Your pair of threes have been **counterfeited** by the appearance of a second pair, higher than yours, on the board. You had the best hand right up to the river, and would have won the pot if the river card had been any 2, 3, 6, 7, 8, 9, 10, J, or Q. Of the 44 cards left in the deck at the turn, 32 would have made you a winner. You got unlucky when the river card was not one of those.

Example 3

This hand is a split pot. Both you and your opponent have a jack-high straight. In fact, neither one of you is playing either of your two

cards. Your opponent had the better hand on the turn with an already made jack-high straight against your 10-high straight, but the jack on the river counterfeited his hand. On the turn, there remained in the deck only two cards that would cause him not to win the pot, and one of those came. That, too, would be considered a bad beat.

Notice that if a third opponent was in the hand holding a queen, he would win the pot.

Example 4

The A-7 wins this pot. His hand is aces full of threes, playing only the ace in his hand. You have fours full of aces, the same hand you had on the turn. If you lose a pot this way (and you will), you are entitled to a bit of grumbling. And notice that your opponent would also have won if an ace or 7 came on the river.

Tip 1

Limit Versus No-Limit Poker

Although the mechanics of limit and no-limit hold'em are the same in that players receive two cards and use them in conjunction with the five **board cards**—community cards, the five cards dealt to the center of the table and shared by each active player—that is pretty much where the similarities stop. Some players are proficient at both forms of poker, but it is a mistake to assume that being a good limit hold'em player automatically makes you effective at no-limit. Here, then, are a few fundamental differences in the two variations:

A. It is rarely, if ever, correct to limp in if no one has yet entered a pot in limit hold'em. However, opening a pot by calling is a viable no-limit play employed by many of the top no-limit players. There are a few reasons for this.

> **1.** It is absolutely essential for a good no-limit player to mix up his play. An occasional limp when first in helps keep your opponents off guard, particularly if you limp with a variety of hands (sometimes two aces, sometimes 8-7 suited).

2. In limit hold'em, if you limp in and are raised, the strongest action you can take when it gets back to you is to reraise one more unit, a play that will only succeed in building a bigger pot that you must then play against the raiser while out of position (unless the raise came from one of the blinds). However, in no-limit hold'em, you can limp in, get raised, and then have the option of reraising as much as you like. This grants your hand considerably more leverage, as well as providing you with an opportunity to really trap your opponents when you are holding a monster hand such as aces or kings.

3. Another incentive to limp is that no-limit hold'em is a game of *implied odds*. **Implied odds** is the ratio of what you should win, including money likely to be bet in subsequent rounds, on a particular hand to what the current bet costs. As a result, it is frequently correct to try to cheaply see a flop with a weaker hand that has the potential to develop into a big hand. An example would be a small pocket pair or a suited ace with a small kicker. These types of hands can capture a big pot if they connect with the flop, but the amount these hands can win in limit hold'em is constrained by the betting structure.

B. How draws are played is much different in no-limit versus limit hold'em. Suppose four people have called before the flop, and you call on the button with A♠ 10♠. Now, the flop comes 6-8-Q, with two spades. In limit hold'em, if everybody checks to you, you can definitely bet this hand. You might make your flush, catch an ace, or have everyone fold.

However, in no-limit, it is far more dangerous to make a bet with this draw. The reason for this is that one of your opponents may make a large check-raise, forcing you to either fold your nut flush draw or make a marginal, or oftentimes bad, call. If you have a short stack, it is fine to bet some or all of your chips with your draw, as you don't mind being committed to this hand. You will either win the pot uncontested (for a small profit), get called and make your hand (for a decent profit), or get called and miss (for a modest loss).

Thus, there is considerable value in betting. However, if you have lots of chips, but make only a fairly small bet on the flop, folding is likely to be the correct play if you get check-raised.

For this reason, it is usually best to take the **free card**—the situation in which there is no bet on a particular round, so players get an extra card without having had to risk additional money—when your stack is **deep**, that is, you have a lot of chips. However, you should bet the draw aggressively when short-stacked. A point to add is that when you are on a short stack, the chips in the middle mean more to your stack than if you have a big stack, so there is more incentive to try to win them right away.

C. You can protect your hand more effectively in no-limit. Since you can make any size bet you want in no-limit, your good hands are less likely to be outdrawn than in limit. This is because you will be able to make large bets that make it difficult for your opponents to remain in the pot.

D. Early in no-limit tournaments, huge implied odds situations exist. No-limit is a game of implied odds. Top no-limit players don't mind seeing a cheap flop with an inferior starting hand in an attempt to catch a lucky flop and double up. The key here is to recognize when your hand has improved enough to merit "going to war." There is a good reason why some hands are inferior—they wind up making the second-best hand quite often. However, as your hand reading skills evolve, you too will be able to see some extra flops hoping to "get lucky." Typical hands that have good implied odds are small pairs and suited aces. With a small pair, if you flop a set against an overpair, you will get paid off handsomely. With a suited ace, you can make aces up against a hand like A-K or A-Q, or, better, a flush. The key here is that a small initial investment can yield a big reward. Although these types of hands can also win some nice pots in limit hold'em, they hold nowhere near the same value as in no-limit.

Tip 2

Adjusting to Your Opponents

One of the most attractive features of no-limit hold'em is that many situations afford considerable flexibility in choosing the best approach. That is, there is more than one path to success. The game is fascinating because, despite its basic simplicity, the situations that can arise within the game can be incredibly complex. This is largely due to the disparity in the quality of play that your opponents demonstrate.

A chief consideration in how you play a hand is how your opponents in the hand play. This is probably of equal or greater importance to your results than the actual cards you are holding. Here are a few guidelines for playing when you find yourself against either poor or very good players.

1. Try to see more flops against weaker players. It should be obvious that you want to play more against inferior players. You will make more money against them with your good hands, and lose less with your bad ones. Even if your opponent starts with a superior hand such as two aces, it's not necessarily a disaster. If you can see a flop for a modest price, you are likely to get all your money into the pot should you outdraw him. However, an excellent player will probably correctly read that you have him beat, thus limiting the amount of your win.

2. Don't slow-play the best hand against excellent players. Although even the best players in the world occasionally fall victim to a cunning and well-laid trap, they certainly will be able to sniff it out much of the time. Also, one strength of most top players is their ability to make good decisions after the flop. Therefore, if you have the opportunity to build a big pot preflop with a big hand, versus waiting until after the flop, you should generally opt to get the money in right away when your opponents are highly skilled. This takes away their implied odds created by their superior postflop play. Don't try to play "small bet poker" against the better players; they will make good decisions that will cost you money whether you win or lose the pot.

3. At a tough tournament table that won't be breaking up for a long time, gamble to try to get some chips. This doesn't mean that you should be playing for all your money as a 4-to-1 underdog. What you should be, though, is willing to play some of the classic "coin flip" situations that frequently come up in no-limit tournaments. These are close to even money shots in which one player is a small favorite with a pair, and the other a small underdog with two overcards. If you are among the strongest players in the tournament, you will want to wait for a bigger edge to play a major pot, as sooner or later your weaker opponents will make a mistake in a big hand. However, at a very tough table that won't be breaking up, it may be to your advantage to play a coin flip in an effort to either double up or get up. If you are fortunate enough to win the hand, you will not only have a good stack, but presumably will have eliminated a tough opponent, paving the way for a more desirable replacement at your table.

4. Move **all in**, that is, bet all your chips, more often against a good player. Good players play well at all points of a hand. If you move all in when you feel you hold the best hand (or when you think your opponent will fold), you remove most of the weapons from your opponent's arsenal. Now, he is forced to decide if he wants to call a big bet, which may cripple or eliminate him should he lose the pot. Often your opponent may feel it will be a coin-flip situation, and opt to wait for an opportunity in which he's a more decided favorite. Unless you run into a huge hand, you will usually win the pot immediately. A word of caution, though. It is nearly always a mistake to move all in when doing so constitutes a huge overbet of the pot. For example, betting $2,000 into a $100 pot is not very smart, as you will be called only when you are way behind.

5. Pick on certain players. All things being equal, you obviously want to play against the weak and passive players at your table. The same is true with any opponents whom you can bluff out of the pot or who are on tilt, playing badly. There's no sense going up against an excellent opponent if you can just as easily face a weaker one.

Tip 3

Knowing the Player Types

Player types are an important aspect of no-limit hold'em. Although no two players are ever the same, player hand selection and betting behavior tend to fall into specific categories.With respect to hand selection, players are either *tight* or *loose*. With betting behavior, they're either *passive* or *aggressive*.

Tight is not playing many hands; having very strict hand selection criteria. **Loose** is playing many hands; having lax hand selection criteria. **Passive** is not initiating many bets; generally preferring to call, as opposed to raising. **Aggressive** is tending to bet and raise frequently and often with large amounts, in preference to calling. Often people confuse passive with tight and loose with aggressive. It's important to understand the distinctions.

When you put the hand selection and betting categories together, the result is four basic player type classifications:

1. **Loose-aggressive**: This describes someone who is loose with his hand selection and aggressive with his betting behavior.

2. **Tight-passive**: This describes someone who is tight with his hand selection and passive with his betting behavior.

3. **Loose-passive**: This describes someone who is loose with his hand selection and passive with his betting behavior.

4. **Tight-aggressive**: This describes someone who is tight with his hand selection and aggressive with his betting behavior. (As you'll learn throughout this book, this is the most effective player type for no-limit hold'em.)

The next four tips cover in-depth strategies for defeating opponents from each of these four classifications.

Tip 4

Beating Loose-Aggressive Opponents

The loose-aggressive player type is often known as a **maniac**. Most players dread this type of opponent because he is erratic, unpredictable, and hard to pin down. The loose-aggressive opponent is the guy who might raise with 2-4 offsuit just because 24 is his favorite number.

Characteristics of a Maniac

Loose-aggressive opponents, maniacs, play a lot of hands (not necessarily good ones) and bet them aggressively. They bluff quite often. Over time, the hands won by loose-aggressive players are those in which everyone else at the table folds, not the showdowns. When a loose-aggressive opponent wins a showdown, it's often the result of a lucky draw.

At first glance, it would seem that loose-aggressive opponents are easy to defeat, but the opposite is the case. The reason is because these players often effectively leverage position, spot weakness at the table, and bully others.

Identifying a Loose-Aggressive Player

Although they're a challenge to defeat, loose-aggressive opponents are easy to spot. They're the ones who enter practically every pot and always seem to represent strong cards.

A key characteristic of loose-aggressive players is their large bet frequency. Good players play aggressively, but loose-aggressive opponents make sizable bets and raises excessively because of their loose starting hand selection criteria.

Beating Loose-Aggressive Opponents

The trick to winning against loose-aggressive opponents is not to try beating them, but to let them beat themselves. The weakness of this player type is that he tries to buy too many pots and makes too many large bets. The secret to defeating him is to be patient and wait for very strong hands that he likely can't beat.

At a full table, wait like you normally would for premium hands and play them aggressively. If the maniac comes in doing the raising for you, just **smooth call**—call, and specifically not raise—on your turn. Don't let him know you've got a **monster**, a very big hand for the situation, such as flopping a set or better. Make him think you've got something decent so that he'll hang on to the hope that he can buy the pot from you.

At a short-handed table against a maniac, you have to play his game. You can't just sit back and be as patient, because the blinds will eat you up. The best tactic is this: If you have a marginal hand, raise him. If you have a strong hand, call.

Don't get yourself into trouble with bad hands. You want the loose-aggressive opponent to come to you when you have the monster.

Keep in mind, however, that even maniacs pick up pocket aces once in a while. Don't automatically assume that just because the raiser is a maniac, he's on a bluff, especially if this is the third time in a row he's raised before the flop. It all depends on the player and situation you're in.

Tip 5

Beating Tight-Passive Opponents

Tight-passive opponents are exactly opposite of loose-aggressive ones. Instead of being a loose cannon, ready to buy the pot and bet aggressively at any given moment, the tight-passive opponent just sits there. That's why this type is commonly known as a **rock**. He gets aggressive only when he's got the nut hand.

Characteristics of a Rock

The primary characteristic of the tight-passive opponent is that he doesn't get involved in many hands. When he does, he generally does not bet them aggressively. When this player has a solid hand, he'll limp in, call a small raise, or possibly make a weak raise. He's generally worried about all the ways he can get beat, as opposed to jumping in and risking chips.

Identifying a Tight-Passive Player

The simplest way to spot a tight-passive opponent is to look for the player who folds on the river, folds to small raises, or folds even when pot odds are in his favor for a call. Also watch for someone who check-calls, because that is typical tight-passive behavior.

Beating a Tight-Passive Opponent

As you probably already figured out, the way to beat this player type is to bet, bet, and bet. When you're aggressive you'll often scare this opponent out—even when he has better cards.

If you ever get raised by a tight-passive opponent and you don't have the stone-cold nuts, run away. Fast!

Tip 6

Beating Loose-Passive Opponents

Of any player type, loose-passive is the least effective and easiest to defeat. This player is sometimes known disparagingly as a **fish**. When you encounter a loose-passive opponent, you can literally turn him into your own personal ATM machine, as long as you know how.

Characteristics of a Loose-Passive Player

Loose-passive opponents are fairly easy to spot because they involve themselves in many pots but are easily scared into folding. On a draw, this player type sticks around when he shouldn't, but then folds if the pressure gets turned up too high.

The nickname **calling station** is often applied to a loose-passive player because he calls many of your bets but rarely raises. If he does make a raise, you're generally better off folding.

When a loose-passive opponent has a good starting hand but doesn't hit on the flop, he usually checks. When he only marginally improves his hand on the flop, he check-calls.

Identifying a Loose-Passive Player

The quickest way to identify the fish at your table is to look for the opponent quickly losing all his chips!

Beating a Loose-Passive Opponent

A loose-passive opponent is the easiest to defeat in no-limit hold'em. Your strategy should be to adopt an aggressive playing style against this opponent. With strong hands, bet an amount such that he'll call you with marginal cards all the way to the river.

A powerful weapon is to simply represent the flop on a consistent basis against the loose-passive player type. Pretend that each flop is terrific for you, because if it wasn't terrific for the fish he'll fold to your bet.

You don't need to be tricky against loose-passive opponents. Just stick to the fundamentals and you'll quickly come out on top.

Tip 7

Beating Tight-Aggressive Opponents

Tight-aggressive opponents are "sharks." Anytime you notice sharks at the table, it might be a good idea to stand up and move somewhere else. After all, there's no sense playing when you're outmatched, if you can avoid the situation!

Chances are, however, you will often be the best player at the table, if for no other reason than having studied this book. In tournaments, you won't be given the luxury to choose your table, so it's best to learn how to defeat the tight-aggressive opponent.

Characteristics of the Tight-Aggressive Player

The tight-aggressive player doesn't waste his money playing bad hands. He's patient and plays premium hands aggressively. He gets his money in the pot with the best hand and protects his money when he doesn't have the best hand.

A tight-aggressive player may see maybe 1 in 5 flops, or maybe only 1 in 10. He folds a lot, but when he sees a flop, he's ready for serious action.

Identifying a Tight-Aggressive Player

Tight-aggressive opponents can be difficult to pinpoint at first glance, but a careful observation of the table will quickly clue you in.

Look for the player who doesn't play a lot of hands, but seems to win a majority of the hands he does play. Especially take notice of the pot size of the hands won by this opponent, because the larger the pot the more likely you've identified a true shark.

Beating Tight-Aggressive Opponents

Ultimately you must learn how to beat good poker players like yourself because that's the only way you'll win serious money in the game.

The way to beat a tight-aggressive opponent is to study for his weaknesses and look for areas in which you're stronger. Ask yourself, does he seem to chase too many draws? Does he give off any **tells**, mannerisms that gives away a player's holdings. Does he fail to make his betting patterns unpredictable?

Your goal is to create situations at the table in which your strengths are matched against his weaknesses, ultimately leading to his defeat.

Tip 8

When to Check-Call

The check-call is generally not an advised play in no-limit hold'em because it limits your control at the table and read on your opponent. There are times, however, when the check-call can be the best play for the situation.

Medium Hands Against a Known Bluffer

If you're up against an opponent who tries to bluff every time he senses weakness, the check-call can be an effective play. The reason is because your check gives him permission to bet aggressively in hopes of stealing the pot. Of course, since you've got a real hand you can call his bet. This allows you to draw more chips from your opponent than you otherwise might have gotten.

Strong Hands Against a Player Who Will Fold to a Bet

It is frustrating to have great cards but face an opponent who will fold to any bet. How can you build the pot to win more chips? The answer often is to check-call, thus giving your opponent control of the betting. You want him to lead the action since he'll lay down his cards if you come out firing.

Stay alert when making a check-call play, especially if you have only a medium-strength hand. Try getting a read on your opponent to make sure he's bluffing or buying the pot, because you don't want to get burnt by a monster. Also be careful if there are visible draws on the board, because you're allowing him to see cards for cheap if he chooses.

Tip 9

Changing Seats

Just as being aware of your position during the play of a hand is a fundamental aspect of hold'em, so too is where you're sitting at the table relative to your opponents. The general rule is that you want the loose players on your right.

The logic behind this strategy is that looser players will often enter more pots and drive the betting. You'll be able to learn more information and predict the outcome of the hand after the loose player has acted. This will be of tremendous importance when timing your bluffs and raises, or when deciding whether to play a marginal hand.

In tournaments, you can't choose where you're sitting at the table, and sometimes you'll end up with loose players on your left. Adjust your strategy accordingly because it will play an important factor in your game. With loose players on your left, you want to let them open up the betting and do the raising for you. When you'd normally consider a bet or raise, consider instead allowing the players to your left to turn up the action.

Be careful when trying to bluff or steal pots under these table conditions, because you'll often not know how your opponents will react. It's oftentimes better to steal pots mainly from the blinds because then your loose opponents have already acted preflop and you've gained the much-needed information.

Tip 10

When to Move All In

In no-limit hold'em, going all in is a very powerful and important move. Luckily, most players don't know the right times to make this bold play. They just wait for the nuts to come along and then they go all in. This tip covers some ideas on how, when, where, and why to go all in.

Not only is this move what makes no-limit poker so exciting, but it is also another key distinction between limit and no-limit hold'em. It's what makes psychology, intimidation, and bluffing so important in no-limit.

As previously discussed, it's better to raise than to call. The same is true with moving all in. It's generally better to make the all-in bet than to call an opponent's all-in move. The reason is because when your opponent goes all in, he has put you to a decision for all your chips. Your life in a tournament could be over with just that one pot.

Just think of it this way: It's much easier to shoot a bullet than to dodge a bullet (and I'm not talking about aces).

To call, you must be confident that you have your opponent beat. On the other hand, in order to make an all-in bet yourself, you just need to be confident that either your opponent will fold or you have him beat. This gives the person making the all-in bet the advantage every time.

So what are the best conditions to make an all-in play?

You Want Outs

If your opponent calls, cards should be left in the deck that can help you still win the hand. Even if the chances aren't great, you want some outs as a backup measure.

You Must Have a Solid Read on Your Opponents

Since you're risking your entire chip stack with an all-in move, you need to be confident in your read on your opponents. If you're not confident they'll fold, or that you have the best hand, don't move all your chips into the middle.

You Want Good Position at the Table

Position is what usually allows you to get a read on your opponents. The better position you have, the more likely you'll be able to successfully steal chips by moving all in.

Be Aware of Stack Sizes

There's always a chance you'll lose an all-in battle. It's much better to lose to a player who has fewer chips than you, because that way you're not eliminated (if it's a tournament). In addition, it's generally easier to bully players with fewer chips, because they know they could be eliminated if they lose to you.

Watch Out for the Short Stack

Here's an important exception to the previous advice. Be careful about stealing pots or making bluffs against a player who is short on chips (with a stack 10 times the big blind or less). This type of player is itching to move all his chips in as soon as he gets any type of hand. That means he'll be much harder to bluff.

On the other hand, if you have a strong hand against the short-stack player, you should be willing to move all in, because he's more likely to make a loose call.

Just be careful in tournaments where other players might also join the pot in hopes of eliminating a player. Often the prospect of removing a player from the table overrides logic and leads to irrational play.

Tip 11

Calling a Preflop Raise With the Worst Hand

This tip is all about *implied odds.* While implied odds are relevant while playing limit poker, their significance in those games is dwarfed by no-limit. What I am talking about here are situations in which you aren't starting with the best hand, perhaps even holding a real long shot. However, should your hand improve to become the best hand, you figure to win a lot of chips.

The big question, then, is what makes a marginal or bad hand worth playing? If you indiscriminately play long-shot hands, you will soon find yourself on the rail or watching the tournament, rather than participating. It is important that you are able to accurately evaluate situations in which the necessary implied odds are present for playing a weak starting hand. This tip should help you develop a framework for making good decisions in this area.

Pick Your Opponents

A key consideration for entering a pot should always be who else is in the hand. Here is an example: One player has raised and now you must decide whether to play a questionable hand. So, ask your-self questions about the raiser. What type of player is he? Is he a good player, one who is raising with a quality holding but won't get married to it if he feels he is behind? If so, you should wait for a better opportunity, and toss your cards into the **muck**, the discard pile. However, if the raiser is likely to go down with the ship, then you should be more apt to play your hand. The reason for this is that suppose you outflop his big pair. A good player might be able to get away from his hand, but many players are incapable of folding aces or kings at any point in the hand. These are the types of players you want to play small pairs or small connectors against, as you will get paid off handsomely when you connect. Thus, the implied odds are there.

Pay Attention to Stack Sizes

Typically, if your opponent moves all in before the flop, you want to play only if you feel your hand is likely the best. This is because there will be no more betting. Implied odds do not apply in this case. However, if you both have lots of chips left, you should be more inclined to call raises less than all in with the worst hand if you feel you might win a huge pot if your hand improves. Probably the best example of these premium implied odds situations is when an op-ponent raises with what you believe is likely to be a high pair. If you call with a small pair and flop a set, you might double your stack.

Don't Risk Too Much of Your Stack on Marginal Situations

The overall value of calling raises with dicey hands can be di-minished by a few factors. First, if your opponent makes a big raise coming in, such that it would require more than 5 percent of your stack to call and see a flop, it is probably best to pass. Higher initial costs hurt your implied odds. Also, when you get short-stacked, you want to wait for either a good hand or a good opportunity to play, as any decision is likely to involve all your chips. There is no point in calling a raise with an inferior hand when short-stacked, as you won't have enough chips left in your stack with which to play post-flop poker to give you the necessary implied odds.

Tip 12

Quick Decisions Are Bad Ones

Anytime you are faced with a major decision in life, be it pur-chasing a new home or automobile, or simply deciding where to travel on vacation, you consider your options. There is no point in making a rushed decision, particularly when the financial or personal consequences of a poor choice can be rather severe.

When playing no-limit poker, it is crucial to your success that you consider all the possibilities prior to making a decision. Acting too quickly can cause you to overlook factors that should be included in your decision-making process. These factors are outlined in the tips ahead.

If you get in the habit of acting quickly, you will find that you often overlook the best course of action. This is not to say that your first impressions are generally incorrect. Quite the contrary will be true as you hone your skills and develop good instincts. Nevertheless, even if your instincts are correct, it doesn't hurt to do a more thorough evaluation of the situation before putting your whole stack—or your tournament life—on the line.

I am not recommending that you **go in the tank**—sit and think for an unusually long time—for several minutes every hand. You know you're folding that 7-2 offsuit, so don't waste everyone's time. However, many important situations come up in no-limit hold'em, particularly in a tournament, and it would be a shame to make a crucial error simply because you didn't take an adequate amount of time to think things through.

One point worth adding here: If you take some time only when faced with a difficult decision, your better opponents will get a read on you. So, occasionally you must mix things up by taking your time to make an obvious decision. This will help keep the pace of your game unpredictable in the eyes of your opponents. The more unpredictable you are, the more difficult it will be for your opponents to play correctly against you.

Tip 13

Knowing Your Outs

Amidst all the complex analysis involved in playing no-limit hold'em tournaments, it can be easy to lose sight of the bottom line: How likely are you to end up with the best hand?

To determine the answer, you should always be aware of how many **outs** (cards that can make your hand the winner) you have.

Your Hand

Board

For example, if you are holding 6♣ 5♣ and the flop comes J-10-9 with two clubs, it's a fairly safe bet that only another club will make your hand the winner. Thus, in this case, your hand has 9 outs (all the remaining clubs).

Another consideration is whether all of your outs are "clean." This refers to the possibility that one or more of the cards that make your hand might make an even better hand for someone else. In the preceding example, any club that also pairs the board might make a full house for an opponent. As your hand reading skills develop with practice, you will become more adept at recognizing when not all of your outs are clean.

Once you have calculated your likely number of outs, it will be fairly apparent whether the necessary pot odds are present for you to remain in the hand. However, until you know how many outs you have, you won't be able to determine whether your hand is worth a call.

Tip 14

Mixing It Up

Great poker players understand the importance of mixing up their bets and raises. It's so simple to do, yet most players fail on this critical point. As I'll discuss later, one of the keys to winning is to identify the betting patterns of your opponents. Of course, your opponents (the smart ones, anyway) will often try to identify your betting patterns. It's your job not to let them!

Be sure to constantly mix up your bets, raises, and betting behavior for different starting hands. This will give you leverage to trick your opponents.

For example, let's say you make an aggressive preflop raise with 6-5 suited after sensing weakness at the table. Everyone folds as you expect, and then you flip over your cards and jokingly say, "C'mon, no one could beat a 6-high?"

Another hour passes and you pick up pocket kings on the button. You make an aggressive preflop raise, similar to the amount before. One of your opponents has K-J and remembers that you made the same preflop raise on a total bluff last time.

So he decides to come **over the top**, make a large raise or re-raise. And to make a long story short, you end up winning all his money. These types of situations won't happen too often, of course, but when they do they'll substantially improve your chip stack.

2 ♣

Tip 15

Be the Raiser, Not the Caller

2 ♣

This tip fits into the overall theme that aggressive play is preferred for no-limit hold'em, especially in tournaments. It is difficult, if not impossible, to have success at this game if your action of choice is the call.

The main reason for this is that by raising, you have two ways to win the pot: You might end up with the best hand or all your opponents might fold. When you call, your only hope is that you can show down the best hand. Simply put, with the large fields in today's no-limit hold'em tournaments, if you think waiting for the best hand to come your way is what it takes to win the tournament, you will be waiting a long time to book a winner. The reason that many of the same faces keep popping up at no-limit final tables isn't that these guys are **human card racks**, players who get a lot of good hands. Nope, the truth of the matter is that they have mastered the art of having two ways to win a hand, and they practice it with a dizzying frequency.

In a tournament, it is particularly important to enter a pot with a raise if you are the first one in. This may enable you to win the blinds and antes without a fight. As a tournament progresses and the blinds are raised, winning the blinds fairly often becomes paramount to your success, as your stack will erode if you fail to grab your share of the money in the pot.

After other players have already entered the pot, you must be more cautious with your raises. Although you should upgrade your raising standards a bit, this doesn't mean you shouldn't at least consider making a raise. If you feel everyone is likely to fold, it is often worthwhile to make a large raise to try to win the money already in the pot. When doing this, however, it is a good idea to note which player initially limped in to the pot. Some players love to slow-play their big pairs, and if one of these players was the first (or even the second) to enter a hand, you should think twice before deciding to raise.

Tip 16

Making the Big Call

O nce in a while, you might just decide to grit your teeth and call with your J-J when someone moves all in. Three main factors are at work here: stack sizes, knowledge of your opponent, and position.

Stack Sizes

In a tournament, if the player moving all in has either a huge or a very small stack, it may be less likely his hand is a monster. Huge stacks may be guilty of bullying with weaker hands, and short stacks (early in the tournament) tend to be reckless with their last few chips. Some players seem to stop caring when their chips get short. Don't be one of them.

Knowledge of Your Opponent

Some players move all in on bluffs, even early in an event, if they think doing so will get you to fold a big hand. You will have to dig your heels in and call these guys if you've identified them.

Position

An opponent is more likely to go all in with a worse hand than yours if he feels you are weak. So, when you raise in early position (indicating strength) and get reraised, it is likely you are up against a legitimate hand. Conversely, your raise on the button is unlikely to be met with the same degree of respect. If one of the blinds reraises you after you have opened the pot from the button, you should be more apt to play.

Tip 17

Knowing What Your Opponents Are Holding

Of all the hands played in a no-limit hold'em tournament, relatively few actually reach a showdown. So, it stands to reason that although the quality of your hand is important, particularly so in hands that reach the showdown, it often doesn't really matter what you have. Whether you have a pair of aces or a 7-2 offsuit, if the hand doesn't reach a showdown, it is all the same to your opponents.

Therefore, it is paramount that you learn to gauge when an opponent is strong, and when he is weak. If you deduce that he is strong, you know that you will need a good hand (and perhaps an exceptional one) to continue playing.

So, how will you know when he is strong? Here are a few factors to consider:

1. What position did he enter the pot from? The worse his position, the stronger his holding is likely to be, unless he is a player who doesn't incorporate position into his thought process.

2. Did he raise, reraise, or call a big bet to enter this pot? Players in raised pots generally have stronger hands than those in limped pots.

3. How loose or tight is your opponent? The more hands he plays or raises, the weaker his starting hand is likely to be.

After weighing the evidence, if you have concluded that your opponent's hand is very strong, you will need to lay down even some of your better hands. It is far better to push weak hands when you feel your opponents are also weak than it is to hang in with strong hands when your opponent is also strong. The exception here, of course, is when your strong hand is either the nuts or close to it.

The importance of this concept cannot be emphasized too strongly. When both you and your opponent are weak, whoever demonstrates the most strength will win the pot. Thus, your cards do not matter; you will win the pot based on your read of your opponent, followed up by a bet on your part. However, when you have a good hand but fear that your opponent does as well, you will have to show down the best hand to take the pot. You may win a large pot this way, but may also find that most or all of your stack will be pushed to your opponent if you can't produce the winner. So, honing your hand reading skills will allow you to recognize situations in which the other players are weak, presenting you with numerous opportunities to pick up pots that are up for grabs.

Tip 18

Study Your Opponents' Betting Patterns

Betting patterns refer to the tendencies of your opponents to play in a consistent, predictable manner. Although the best no-limit players are able to mix up their game to a degree that makes them highly unpredictable, most players are fairly easy to peg. These are the players whom you should be looking to play most of your hands against, as their predictable style of play will allow you to make better decisions against them.

Continuing with the theme of hand-reading, here is a list of items to be aware of in studying the betting patterns of your opponents:

1. How does position influence which hands your opponents play? Does your opponent play great hands only when out of position, or could he have a wide range of hands? Also, how much do your opponents loosen up when in good position?

2. Does an opponent consistently make big bets on his good hands, and smaller bets on weaker hands? Or, is the situation reversed?

You have less to fear from some players if they move all in than if they make a smaller wager. It is important to identify what the size of a bet tells you about a particular opponent's holding.

3. Does an opponent always bet if it's checked to him in last position? Many players fall into this category, and it is valuable to know and exploit this pattern in an opponent.

4. When does an opponent check-raise? Some players need a huge hand to check-raise, while others often make this play with a straight or flush draw. Know where your opponents fit in the check-raising spectrum.

5. How does an opponent proceed with his drawing hands? Does your opponent bet draws aggressively, or are draws strictly check-and-call types of hands to them? Also, some of your opponents are prepared to go all the way with a flush or straight draw, while others will fold without much of a fight. It is helpful to know which type of opponent you are up against.

Tip 19

Winning in
Heads-Up Play

Heads-up play is one of the most important and underdeveloped skills for most no-limit hold'em players. But, to win first place in any given tournament or prevail in any game, you must win the heads-up matches. The problem is that most players don't find themselves in heads-up situations frequently enough to practice and perfect the skill. Oftentimes heads-up matches last only a few hands (because of the blinds), which isn't nearly enough time to learn the art of winning one-on-one.

Let's take a look at what it takes to become a dominating heads-up player.

Bet Often

You cannot and will not win at heads-up poker if you play only premium cards. The reason is simple: For most hands, neither you nor your opponent will catch anything good. It's simple mathematics.

That means you've got to win by making your opponent fold, and the way to accomplish this is through betting.

Show the Occasional Bluff

This technique is optional, but can be very powerful in the right situations. Heads-up poker is largely dependent on psychology and intimidation, so it's smart to make actions that will confuse and scare your opponent.

You don't have to show a bluff to achieve this desired effect. You simply need to mix up your game and betting patterns to remain unpredictable. Your opponent will be studying you for any signs of consistency.

Control the Pace

By assuming control of the tempo of the heads-up match, you can also influence the stakes you play at. For instance, if the blinds in a heads-up match are low, the match can go for a really long time, a really short time, or somewhere in between. It all depends on the players.

Some players will start pushing all in with any ace, pair, or other decent-looking hand as soon as they reach heads-up. Other players prefer to play the heads-up match more slowly.

So which way is better? The answer is whichever way works best for you and leads most often to wins. That's precisely why you want to be the one who takes control.

Give Your Opponent a False Sense of Hope to Set a Trap

If you've stolen pots from your opponent with your aggressive betting, and perhaps **tilted him**—cause him to play poorly and irrationally due to emotional upset—by showing a bluff, it's time to back down and give him a feeling of hope. This is designed to set a trap. Try adopting a few betting patterns that are fairly easy to recognize. (Of course, your opponent will feel like he's discovered a "secret" when he notices them.) Stop mixing up your game as much and instead become intentionally predictable. Your opponent will gain a false sense of hope that he really can defeat you, when in reality you're simply setting a trap.

Let Your Opponent Make the Wrong Move

Once your trap is set, it's time to let your opponent walk in. With a strong hand for instance, play it exactly the way you've been playing your weaker hands. Since your opponent will think he's figured out your betting patterns, he'll bet and raise with looser hand requirements.

The result is you'll be able to trap him into becoming **pot-committed**—having put so much money into a pot that he feels obligated to play the pot to the end—and you'll gain a large stack by winning a major pot.

Practice Your Heads-Up Skills Often

The most effective way to become a winning heads-up player is to practice often. Invite a poker buddy over to play several hours of consecutive matches. This will help develop your intuition and understanding of the nuances in heads-up strategy. Or play online poker, where you will find many tables devoted to heads-up play.

Tip 20
Spotting Bluffs

One key principal to keep in mind when deciding if someone, particularly an unsophisticated or relatively inexperienced player, is bluffing or has a great hand is that players are often acting, and they act in a manner opposite to the strength of their hand. If a player acts strong, he is probably weak. If a player acts weak, he is probably strong.

Mike Caro was the first to put this amazing insight into words many years ago. As you'll discover, almost every poker tell boils down to this fundamental principle.

Let's discuss how you can use this concept to spot bluffs quickly and consistently:

Look for Signs of Both Strength and Weakness

Many players look only for tells that suggest an opponent is bluffing, which is only half of the equation. To get an accurate read on an opponent, you must also look for signs of strength.

Spotting Weakness

Remember that if a player acts strong, he is often weak. This means that when a player does something on the surface that makes it look like he's got a monster hand, he's probably bluffing. Most players don't try to act strong, they simply do it unconsciously.

For example, let's pretend you hold 9-2 offsuit and decide to make a bold bluff by going all in before the flop (obviously not a recommended move!).

Anyway, in your mind you're thinking, "I sure hope no one calls," but when someone starts contemplating a decision, you really start to get worried. So what do you do? The natural thing to do is to act like you're not afraid. Obviously you don't want someone to know that you're scared of getting called, right?

So you sit up straight, your hands don't tremble, and your voice has a little arrogance to it. Ultimately, these are all signs that you're bluffing. You didn't necessarily mean to act this way; it just happened naturally.

Spotting Strength

Now let's reverse this and explore how you can know when an opponent holds a strong hand. As I stated earlier, if a player acts weak, he is probably strong. Acting weak is usually more subtle than acting strong. It's often demonstrated in a way of disinterest.

Once again, the player doesn't usually mean to act weak, it's simply a natural mechanism. A few ways to spot strength is to look for a player who looks away from the table or doesn't make eye contact with you. An opponent who stares you down is frequently bluffing, whereas someone who looks the other direction frequently holds strong cards.

Another sign of strength is an opponent who has suddenly become very quiet after being generally talkative at the table. He's likely praying for you to call his bet, so beware!

Obviously there are exceptions to every one of these cases, and highly skilled poker players often intentionally act weak when they are weak to fool opponents who understand the logic just discussed. Also, many expert players either have no tells at all or their seemingly revelatory mannerisms have no correlation with the cards they're holding. Don't base your decisions on tells you think you've spotted, but instead use this tip as an additional way to get reads on your opponents.

Tip 21

Position Is Crucial

Virtually every book written on poker includes at least some discussion on the merits of position. Obviously, this is an important concept. Exactly how, though, does your position affect you in a no-limit hold'em game?

When you enter a pot in early position (with several players yet to act behind you), you put yourself at a severe disadvantage. First, you don't have a good assessment of the strength of your opponents' hands at this point. Suppose you are holding a reasonable hand like A-J. It may well be the best hand, but you don't yet know this to be true. As a result, if you opt to enter the pot and another player then raises, you can generally be confident that your A-J is trailing. Depending on the size of the other player's raise, you may have to fold. So, you have invested chips in the pot and are then forced to concede them. Playing too many hands out of position results in this happening with an alarming frequency.

Now, suppose you get to look at the flop with your A-J, but there are players who will be acting behind you. This also causes a severe handicap to your hand as the hand plays out. You will be obligated to act before them on each succeeding round of betting, which provides some unpleasant realities for your hand. One is that it will be difficult to win full value on your hand when you do flop a pair, as betting into a few opponents when a scare card (an overcard to the jack, or a card that completes a potential straight or flush) hits is a dubious proposition. Also, many pots in no-limit hold'em go not necessarily to the best hand, but to the aggressor. It is more difficult to take an assertive role when several other hands are yet to act, as you don't have an accurate assessment of their strength.

When you are last to act, however, you can win extra pots simply by making a modest bet when the action is checked to you. Occasionally you will be check-raised or run into a big hand, but you should win enough extra pots with the maneuver to offset this.

As another example, you hold a decent hand like top pair, fair kicker (such as Q-J with a board of Q-10-8-5-4. With a hand like this, it would be difficult to bet for value into a few opponents on the river. However, you may be able to bet if it is checked to you in last position. So, position is especially key when determining whether to play marginal hands that are likely only to make one big pair, due to the common occurrence in which you must decide whether to bet the hand for value. Position is of slightly less importance for hands that seem to play themselves (ones that are extremely powerful) after the flop.

Your Hand

Board

Tip 22

Playing From the Blinds

Playing from the blinds is a delicate balance of knowing your opponents, taking odds into consideration, and closely watching chip stacks—your opponents as well as your own. Implement these strategies and you'll be on your way to more success from these crucial positions.

Following are seven strategies to consider when playing from the blinds.

1. Be Inclined to Call When There Are Many Players in the Pot

Since you've already invested a portion of chips into the pot, it makes sense to see more flops when there are a lot of players in. The pot odds and implied odds are both favorable, assuming there wasn't a large preflop raise.

2. Reraise the Pot if You Think You Can Force the Raiser Out

The blinds offer you the advantage of late position before the flop. If an opponent raises the pot but you suspect he is relatively weak, be willing to attack with a reraise. If the raiser is generally passive but you don't feel comfortable reraising, just call and outplay the opponent after the flop.

3. Fold if the Raiser Tends to Play Only Strong Hands

Don't fall in love so much with your invested blinds that you lose sight of your hand strength. If a tight opponent who generally plays only pairs or aces enters the pot with a raise, you must be willing to lay your weaker hand down. This is especially true since you're likely to act first after the flop.

4. Call More Often When You Have a Large Chip Stack

With a large chip stack you can afford to see more flops, because you're more likely to win after the flop. Use your chip advantage to bully opponents and steal pots from them.

5. Don't Be Afraid to Move All in When You're Short-Stacked

Being short-stacked from the blinds is a good place to make an all-in move because you've gotten the opportunity to witness the betting behavior of your opponents. Your all-in move will likely either win you the pot outright or put you in a coin-flip situation on the flop. This is a great approach to coming back from the short stack.

6. Raise From the Blinds When You Want to Narrow the Field of Opponents

For example, if you have a strong pocket pair, you don't want many players seeing the flop. That makes you less susceptible to being outdrawn. Therefore, with strong hands you want to raise the pot from the blinds and narrow the field to just a caller or two.

Call With Hands When You Want Many Players to See the Flop

If you have holecards that are not strong by themselves, but are great if turned into a made hand, then you generally want multiple players to see the flop to build pot size later.

Suited connectors—two cards in sequence and in the same suit, usually with reference to holecards, for example, 8♠ 9♠—are the perfect example of this. By themselves, your suited connectors won't take down a pot at the showdown, which is why you don't want to invest too many chips before the flop. But if your suited connectors turn into a made straight or flush, it's very likely you'll win in a showdown situation. That's why you want to call the blinds to see a cheap flop and hope to hit a monster.

Tip 23

Playing From the Dealer Position

A large number of the hands you win over the course of a poker game should come when the button is sitting directly in front of you. Having the button means that you're the dealer, the best position at the table. It's the best position because you get to see how a single opponent behaves after the flop before acting. Here's how to capitalize on this positional advantage.

Relax Your Starting Hand Selection Standards

Your preflop hand selection should be loosest from the dealer position and tightest from first position preflop.

Play More Aggressively and Take Control of the Betting

The best way to leverage the button is to control the betting. When you make strong bets and raises, your opponents will often fold to you (because you have the dominating position) or check the next card. The latter gives you the opportunity to see the turn and river possibly for free, which can be a powerful technique if you're on a draw or don't have a made hand.

Change Up Your Play From the Button

Any decent poker player understands the importance of the button. If you adopt the same aggressive behavior every time from this position, your style will quickly become transparent and you'll likely get burnt. Mix up your play.

The goal is not to bet or raise from the dealer position every time you're there. Instead, you want the sum of your actions from this position to be looser and more aggressive than your actions from the other positions at the table.

Tip 24

First Position, Before the Flop

The first position before the flop is the player who is sitting immediately to the left of the big blind. This position is perhaps the hardest position to play at the entire table. That's probably why this position is known as **under the gun**.

After the flop, this is still an early position (assuming you're at an eight-handed table or larger), which makes things worse. Your strategy for playing first position preflop is to stick to premium hands. Don't play the same starting hands as you'd normally play in other positions, otherwise you'll unnecessarily waste chips.

The most obvious reason first position is undesirable is because you don't know what the players behind you will do. You haven't had a chance to get a read on them since you're first to act. If you call the blinds (limp) with a mediocre hand, for instance, you'll often be forced to fold when someone raises. If you raise with a decent starting hand, you'll often have a difficult decision to make when an opponent reraises you.

Stick to starting hands like A-A, K-K, Q-Q, J-J, 10-10, 9-9, A-K, A-Q, K-Q, and small pocket pairs on occasion.

If you're sitting at a tight table and you get a premium hand under the gun, generally the best course of action is to raise. If the table at which you're sitting is aggressive, consider just calling. At an aggressive table someone else will often make the preflop raise for you, which gives you an opportunity to reraise or smooth call. At a tight table you cannot risk letting too many players see the flop because then your chances of winning are decreased dramatically.

Remember that preventing yourself from losing big hands is oftentimes more important than winning big hands. Playing first position before the flop improperly often results in losing large pots, so be careful.

Tip 25

First Position, After the Flop

Being first to act after the flop is a tricky position to play because you're not sure of whether the flop improved any of your opponents' hands. Do you come out firing or do you check? The answer depends on several factors.

How Many Players Saw the Flop

The number of players who see a flop is directly proportional to the chances that someone has a strong holding. If your hand didn't improve, it's generally wise not to bet with multiple players behind you.

Preflop Behavior

If you made a preflop raise, it might be smart to represent the flop with a bet. Good no-limit hold'em players often represent the flop after making a preflop raise, regardless of what hits. The reason goes back to our discussion earlier that it's easier to raise than to call. Your opponents will tend to respect your postflop bet more since you also made the preflop raise.

Obviously there are other considerations and exceptions to this wisdom, such as how many players called your preflop raise, the table image you've established, and the player types of those who saw the flop with you.

Stack Sizes

If you have a dominating chip stack size, you can afford to represent the flop from first position and try to bully your opponents. On the other hand, if your stack size is smaller than the average and the flop didn't help your hand, it might be wiser to stay out of the action and patiently wait for better cards.

Tip 26

Late Position

Late position is much better than early position. If you're in a game with eight to ten players, the button and two seats to its right are considered late position. It is from these seats that you want to play more pots than usual and you should have better-than-average results.

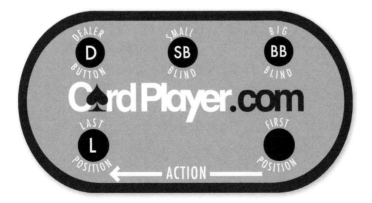

Poker is about decision-making. And, as in the real world in which it is easier to make proper decisions with better data, the same holds true in poker. From late position you have the advantage all four rounds to see what the others do before you have to act.

Take advantage of your position to play more hands, especially when you can play your marginal ones for a small wager.

Tip 27

Playing A-K

Ace-king (or **big slick**, as many call it) is probably the most pivotal hand in no-limit hold'em tournaments. For one thing, there are more combinations of A-K available than other big playable hands such as A-A or K-K. With four aces and four kings in the deck, you have 16 ways to be dealt big slick, while only six combinations of pocket aces exist. So, situations in which a player has A-K arise frequently in tournaments.

A-K is a hand that tournament players like to gamble with. Since only A-A and K-K are decided favorites over A-K, the hand usually gives you a fair gamble. When a lot of money is already in the pot, it is frequently correct to push hard with A-K to try either to win what is already in the pot or "flip a coin" if you are called. When you make a big raise with A-K and are called, you will frequently be up against a medium-to-largish pair such as J-J or Q-Q, hands that are only small favorites over A-K. However, the presence of the blinds, antes, and possibly other money in the pot can make it a profitable situation to gamble with A-K even when you won't win quite half the battles.

Here are a few guidelines to help recognize when it is correct to play a big pot with A-K, and when to play it more conservatively:

Don't Build a Big Pot Preflop With A-K When You Still Will Have Plenty of Chips Left for Betting

This relates to the concept of implied odds. The main value of A-K is that it often makes a pair, and when it does, it is the top pair with the best possible kicker. This is usually enough to win the pot. So, A-K is a hand that can easily improve to make the best hand. Also, A-K sometimes wins unimproved. The problem with A-K is that one pair is typically all it will make, and although it will be top pair, it can lose to a big hand such as two pair or a set.

When both you and your opponent have lots of chips left to bet on the flop, the following scenarios tend to happen with A-K:

1. You flop a pair, bet, and win the pot; or get called for a modest amount when your opponent flops a pair with a worse kicker.

2. Neither of you flops a pair, and whoever makes a bet wins the pot (probably you).

3. You miss, your opponent hits the flop, bets, and wins.

4. You flop a pair and your opponent hits his pocket pair for a set.

Scenario 1 is quite common, demonstrating why A-K is a powerful, high probability hand. Scenarios 2 and 3 are both relatively harmless results. However, scenario 4 is a recipe for disaster, highlighting exactly why A-K is a poor implied odds hand. When you flop top pair, top kicker, it will be difficult for you to release your hand, particularly if the pot is already quite large. When you flop a pair and your opponent flops a set or two pair, you are bound to lose a lot of chips. And, this is the only plausible scenario in which your opponent will put in a lot of money after the flop when an ace or king is present.

I recommend keeping the pot small with A-K when your stack is deep. This way, you won't be as committed to the pot even when you do flop a pair. Also, by not reraising, you help disguise the strength of your hand, and might actually get some action when you flop a pair against a player with a weaker kicker.

A-K Is a Good Hand to Go All in With When You Are Short-Stacked

The reason for this is that your hand is dominated only by A-A and K-K. Against all other hands, you are either a favorite or a small underdog (against pocket pairs). And, if you are all in, you will often be called by a player holding an ace with a worse kicker, putting you in nice shape to double up. The problem of A-K and poor implied odds doesn't apply when all the money is in the pot before the flop, so you don't have to worry about flopping a pair against another player's set. Sure, you'll still lose when this happens, but you got your money into the pot before this happened, when you had a fair shot of winning. The disaster is when you get all in after the flop, holding very few outs.

A-K Is Tricky to Play After the Flop

The good news about A-K is that you are rarely in that bad shape before the flop. Only A-A and, to a much lesser degree, K-K dominate the hand, and you are often in the nice position of playing against an ace with a worse kicker. Unfortunately, A-K is very tricky to play after the flop. This is a genuine concern early in a tournament, when players typically have lots of chips left in their stacks to bet, even after a preflop raise or two.

After the flop, A-K is a hand that typically either wins a small pot or loses a big one. Suppose you catch a nice flop—A-8-3. So, you bet. Although A-Q may pay you off, anyone holding a pocket pair will now fold, acknowledging the presence of the ace on the board.

Your Hand

Board

They will fold, that is, unless their pair is 8-8 or 3-3. Now, you are the one who is trapped. This particular scenario is a common recipe for early elimination.

My advice is to readily fold A-K early on when faced with having to call a big bet if you still have lots of chips for playing after the flop should you call. This will help you avoid the "win a small one, lose a big one" trap.

A-K Tends to Be an Unprofitable Hand Early in Tournaments, But a Good One Later on

Early on in a tournament, you will win a lot of small pots with A-K, either because you are not called or you flop a pair and take the pot. However, you may lose a big one when you flop a pair against a set. Late in the event, the blinds and antes are quite significant, and it is usually correct to try to grab them at every opportunity. So, you shouldn't mind raising and reraising with A-K, as you might win what's already in the pot, and if the hand is contested, you'll usually have a good shot to win anyway.

Tip 28

Playing a Suited Ace

Ace-x* suited is another hand that has value because of the implied odds potential. You have a chance to make the nut flush with this hand, and can often win a big pot when you are successful in doing so, particularly if another player has a flush as well. It is best not to play this hand too strongly before the flop; you want to get in cheaply and not shut out opponents who might make second-best hands. Typically, if you do raise, all you will accomplish is narrowing the field down to you and the best hand, which might be a player holding an ace with better kicker. This is not what you have in mind when you enter a pot with this sort of hand.

Therefore, when all you hit on the flop is one pair, you need to proceed with extreme caution. If you flop a pair of aces, you may be

---

* **x:** Shorthand for any unspecified card. A-x, for example, means an ace plus any other card. A-x suited is an ace plus any other card of the same suit.

in severe *kicker trouble*, and are almost certainly beaten if there is much action. **Kicker trouble** is having an inferior kicker (side card) to a likely better kicker held by another player. For example, if you have A-2 and an ace appears on the board, if there is any betting, there is a good chance that at least one opponent has an ace with a better kicker.

If you're in kicker trouble, you should either check and see what kind of action there is, or make a small "probing" bet, to help define where you stand in the hand. Typically, if you're doing all the betting, there is a fairly good chance your pair of aces is good; however, if you get raised, you are in trouble and should usually abandon ship.

When you flop a smaller pair, it is also important to not get overly excited. You can easily be trailing to a higher pair, or at least in danger of losing to overcards on either the turn or river. Again, you don't want to commit too many chips. In fact, it may be best to hope the hand gets checked around. This way, should you catch a miracle ace on the turn, you will make aces-up, and might get a lot of action from someone who holds a hand like A-Q.

Remember, when you play a suited ace type of hand, you are playing to make something better than one pair. If you proceed with this mentality, you should avoid losing a big pot with A-x. However, don't hesitate to make small bets frequently after the flop, as you can win some small pots this way.

Tip 29

Playing Suited Connectors

Suited connectors can become some of your biggest money makers over the course of a game. These hands are great to raise with or call a raise with because your opponents will never be able to put you on a hand if you hit. What you're hoping to catch on the flop is an open-ended straight draw, a flush draw, or possibly both. Since your opponents will usually not be able to figure out your cards, the implied odds are once again very high in this situation. Follow these considerations when you're holding suited connectors.

Base Your Preflop Betting on Your Position and Stack Size

Since suited connectors don't turn into a made hand very often, you want to play them primarily from late positions at the table and with a comfortable stack size. If your stack is smaller than 15 times the big blind, it's generally unwise to enter a pot with suited connectors.

Bet or Raise on an Open-Ended Straight Draw

If you flop an open-ended straight draw, it's usually best to lead out betting or raising. This action will help you gain control of the table, which often leads to seeing a free card on the river. Additionally, your raise sets the stage for taking down the pot if you miss your draw, because you represented a made hand on the flop.

Be Careful of Flush Draws

Having a flush draw with suited connectors is a dangerous situation for two reasons. First, someone at the table can easily hold a higher flush draw than you. Second, actually making your flush requires there to be three cards of the same suit on the board, which often gives away your hand to opponents.

In the first case, you must be cognizant of the strength of your flush draw and not commit too heavily to the pot with a weak top card. For the second case, you may try to gain control of the betting early on to represent a made hand, depending on several conditions like position, preflop betting behavior, number of opponents, and stack sizes. Your goal is to not make your bets and raises transparent to opponents, so that when the card that makes your hand hits, your opponents don't immediately fold.

Tip 30

Playing Low and Middle Pocket Pairs

This tip covers low (2-8) and middle (9-10) pocket pairs. I exclude J-J here because they're covered in more detail in the next tip. Your strategy for playing pocket pairs largely depends on table conditions. The number of players at the table, your positioning, and your stack size determine how to play these hands both preflop and postflop.

With a Small Pair, You Want to Make a Set

When you play small pocket pairs, most often (unless you're playing short-handed) the desired effect is to make a set. Not doing so will often lead to folding the hand and not committing too many chips. The odds against flopping a set are approximately 7.5-to-1. Although more than 7 of 8 times will result in a miss, pocket pairs are one of the most profitable hands in no-limit hold'em because a set is so difficult to detect.

See the Flop Inexpensively

From early positions, try to see an inexpensive flop with a small pocket pair. It's not generally wise to raise or call any substantial raises with small pocket pairs. The reason is simply mathematics. You will not complete a set often enough to justify committing the extra chips.

You Can Win the Pot With a Middle Pair Without Improvement

With a middle pocket pair, decide whether you want to attempt winning the hand without completing a set. Middle pairs can often win a hand at showdown under the right conditions. With a comfortable stack size and few players in the pot, you can consider making a preflop raise with a hand like 10-10.

Your pocket tens have three different ways of winning: First, you might complete your set. Second, your tens might be the strongest hand at showdown,especially if the flop is rags. Third, by assuming control before the flop you can often win the pot outright with a post-flop bet, not letting the hand go to showdown.

Play a Pair Aggressively in Late Position

From late position, either call a small raise or raise the pot if your opponents all try limping in. If you sense weakness at the table from a late position, do not be afraid to play your pocket pair aggressively. Against two overcards your pair is slightly favored. By taking control and narrowing the action to one or two callers, you can often take the pot after the flop without completing your set. If you get reraised, it's probably better to muck your cards and live to see another hand.

Bottom Line for Pocket Pairs

Obviously you do not want to risk too many chips in these types of situations, but under the right circumstances a pocket pair can be played aggressively because it can win at showdown and has huge implied odds if a set is made by the river.

Tip 31

Playing Pocket Jacks

Pocket jacks are pretty when you look down at them, but often lead to huge losses. Learn to play this hand correctly and you'll save yourself many headaches down the road.

First, it can be helpful to treat a hand like J-J as a drawing hand; that is, one that needs improvement to win the pot. Of course, you will often win with J-J on its own merits. Viewing it as a hand in need of a third jack, though, may help prevent you from putting too much money in the pot when you are trailing. Typically, if three small cards flop and you hold J-J, if an opponent is willing to either make or call a big bet, he is likely to have you beat.

Conventional wisdom holds that since J-J is vulnerable, it is important to play it strongly preflop in order to protect it. Your desire would be to narrow the field to just one or two callers. The problem with this approach is that when you do get action, you are likely to be up against a better hand or A-K, to which you are only a modest favorite.

Consider playing J-J for only a small raise, or by simply calling an opponent's raise. This way, you disguise your hand a bit, and might really win a big pot should you hit your draw (a third jack). Also, you have kept the pot smaller, making it easier to escape when you feel you are beat.

You can choose to play J-J the traditional way and bet aggressively before the flop, but make sure other favorable conditions are present if you do so. These conditions can include, but are not limited to, good position, a solid read on your opponents, and a chip lead. Raking in the blinds and not getting preflop action with J-J can be considered successful, especially in the late stages of a tournament where winning blinds becomes a crucial strategy.

Tip 32

Playing Pocket Queens and Kings

This tip covers techniques for maximizing your winnings with pocket queens and kings, two hands that any hold'em player is delighted to see when he picks up his cards.

Be Aggressive Before the Flop

Kings or queens are difficult to improve on the flop. Since making a set won't happen too often, it's important that you protect these preflop monsters from weak hands that hit on the flop. Make your preflop raise enough to scare away hands like suited connectors and low pocket pairs.

Raise More Preflop With Queens Than With Kings

This isn't a rule that you must always follow, of course, but it leads to better success when adhered to. In general, be more aggressive with pocket queens because they are vulnerable to face-card combinations involving a king.

You want your preflop raise to force out an opponent who's holding something like K-J or K-Q, so that if a king hits on the flop you'll have better odds of still being ahead.

Be Willing to Fold

It's very common for players to be eliminated from an event because they were unwilling to fold pocket queens or kings, even though all logic would have led to this decision.

If you play Q-Q and K-K correctly, an opponent who sees a flop with you often has an ace. If a dreaded ace hits the flop, proceed with extreme caution. This situation is bound to happen from time to time (more often than we'd certainly like) and you must be willing to throw away your cards.

Of course, that's not to say you should immediately give up as soon as an ace hits the board. Your opponent could easily have called your preflop raise with a lower pocket pair, in which case you are still in the dominating position.

Know Your Opponents

Apart from an opponent making a higher pair from the board, your Q-Q and K-K are vulnerable to made sets, flushes, straights, and someone starting with pocket aces.

Losing big pots in these types of situations are almost inevitable over time. You can offset these losses, however, by knowing your opponents. Being attentive throughout the game to how your opponents play their monster hands will clue you in when you run into a monster.

A truly masterful poker player frequently knows when to fold his queens or kings before the flop, by having an incredible read on his opponents.

Tip 33

Playing Pocket Aces

A pair of aces is the best possible starting hand in hold'em. This hand is far less vulnerable than Q-Q and K-K because no one can have a higher pair than you, but, as any experienced poker player will tell you, that doesn't mean it's invincible. You can easily lose all your chips with A-A if you're not careful.

Your approach with A-A should be fairly straightforward: Raise the pot aggressively preflop to narrow the field to one or two callers, then keep betting if nothing too scary hits the board.

Amateur poker players sometimes think that since A-A is the best starting hand, it is desirable to have as many players participating in the pot as possible. The exact opposite is true. The reason is because the more opponents who see a flop, the more likely it is that your aces will be run down by a complete hand.

Before the flop, you would ideally like to get as many of your chips as possible into the middle against one caller. Your opponent will likely have something like A-K, A-Q, K-K, or Q-Q, all of which are dominated by your aces.

If more than one opponent sees a flop with you, be careful if the board creates an obvious straight or flush draw. In these types of situations you can either choose to exit the hand altogether when faced with a large bet, or possibly raise your opponent into a decision in which pot odds do not warrant a call.

Tip 34

Folding Good Preflop Hands in Tournaments

Although it doesn't happen very often, there are situations in which folding good hands such as Q-Q, J-J, or A-K preflop is correct. First let's discuss the pairs. Early in a tournament, most of your opponents will be unwilling to move all in before the flop without one of two hands—A-A or K-K. So, if they raise, you reraise, and then someone moves all in, it is highly likely your Q-Q is no good. You will have plenty of time to find a better opportunity to gamble, so fold. You should be even more inclined to fold J-J, as this hand is trumped by Q-Q as well, a hand some players move all in with early on in a tournament (a play I don't recommend you make).

Sometimes you will fold the best hand when you lay down Q-Q or J-J to an all-in reraise. Most of the time the all-in player has A-K when this happens, a hand that is a very slight underdog (less than 6-to-5), so you aren't giving up too much. Early in the event is not the time to take a stand.

Tip 35

Avoiding Trouble Hands in Tournaments

If A-K has the disadvantage of winning small pots and losing big ones, other hands are even worse off. These trouble hands have the additional burden of being dominated by A-K. Examples include A-Q, A-J, and K-Q. Holding one of these hands, you now lose not only to sets when you flop top pair, but to A-K as well (or to A-Q if you hold A-J). It is going to be very difficult to win anything meaningful after the flop with these hands when they improve in the most common way (making a pair), but easy to make a second-best hand.

There is a sort of reverse implied odds factor at work here. What seemed like a cheap opportunity to see a flop becomes an expensive problem when you improve to a second-best hand. Small pairs typically lose small pots and win big ones, but two high cards typically do the opposite.

The time that trouble hands do have some value is later in the tournament, when the blinds are high and you can get most or all of your chips into the pot before the flop. You still don't have a premium hand, but you don't face the sticky situation of betting after the flop. These hands fare far better in **race situations**—a hold'em confrontation of two closely matched hands, usually with one of the players all in, such as 7♣ 7♦ against A♠ K♥ (the pair is about a 55-45 favorite)—in which the money is all in and the board cards are run out, than they do when the hand must be played on every **street** (preflop, flop, turn, and river).

A **race situation** is a hold'em confrontation of two closely matched hands, usually with one of the players all in. Two overcards against a pair is a classic race situation. For example, in the matchup of 7♣ 7♦ against A♠ K♥, the pair is about a 55-45 favorite.

Tip 36

Betting When You Flop the Probable Best Hand

Suppose it is early in a no-limit tournament, and four players have seen the flop, either for a call or a very modest raise. The flop is favorable to your hand; you are holding either an overpair to the board, or the top pair with a very good kicker. It appears that you are holding the best hand, and the action is on you.

Generally speaking, it is correct to bet close to the size of the pot if you feel you hold the best hand at this point. By making a healthy bet, you are likely to eliminate long-shot draws that may catch you by surprise, such as an inside straight draw. While flush draws may call anyway, you will know to be cautious if a third suited card appears on the board.

Although a pot-sized bet will eliminate most of the draws, anyone else holding top pair is likely to call. This is a good situation for you as you have him drawing to three outs should both of you hold the same pair, but you have the better kicker, or five outs if you hold an overpair. Betting your hand strongly allows you to get full value for it from inferior one-pair hands while protecting yourself against drawing hands that are not getting the proper price to call.

If you are first to act, you can consider the merits of betting out with a good hand versus check-raising. In general, it is probably best to bet most of the time, for two reasons. First, you don't want to give a free card to someone who can outdraw you with a hand he would have folded to a bet. This can end up costing you a lot of money on the turn if the turn card looks harmless. Second, if your hand is just one pretty good pair, you have a good but not great hand. If you lead out with a pot size bet, you gain considerable information about where you stand in the hand. You may gain the same information by check-raising, but you will probably have to invest more chips to do so, as you must call your opponent's bet prior to putting in your own raise. Unless you are fairly positive your one pair is the best hand and that your opponent will bet, you should typically opt to just bet out.

Tip 37

Raising With Draws

Let's discuss how you can win more money with drawing hands. Most players who find themselves on draws will continually check-call their opponents, hoping to complete their hand. This is an expensive and inefficient approach to draws.

An often better method for drawing hands is to raise the pot and gain control of the betting. (It's important that you make a substantial raise, as discussed further in the next tip.)

Raising on a draw accomplishes several important objectives.

Strength of Opponent's Hand

Raising on a draw helps you get a read on the strength of your opponent's hand. By raising an opponent, you force him to a decision, which is the best way to gauge the strength of his hand. If he calls your raise, you know he is solid. If he reraises, you know you are in trouble. If he folds, you've won the pot.

Additional Way to Win

Raising on a draw gives you an additional way to win. If you raise on your straight and flush draws and take control of the betting, you've set yourself up for the opportunity to take the pot down without making your hand. This is especially important, since most of the time you will not catch one of your outs.

By representing a made hand on the flop when you have a draw, you'll have an edge over opponents. If you sense weakness in response to your raise you can take down the pot with a more aggressive bet or raise on the next card.

Your Hand Is Disguised

An additional benefit of representing a made hand is that your true hand is disguised and you're more likely to get paid off when you hit.

For example, let's say you're holding J-10 and the flop hits 9-8-2 rainbow. If you check-call the flop, a queen comes on the turn, and you come out firing, your opponent might be suspicious of the straight. But if you represented the flop when you had the open-ended draw, your opponent won't be as likely to suspect the straight when the queen hits.

Your Hand

Board

Free Card

Raising often buys you a free card. When you raise on a draw, your opponent will often check the next card to you when you have the better position. This gives you the option to do one of the following: You can check, thus getting a free card and improving your chances of making your hand. You can also bet, in hopes of winning the pot outright. The action you choose depends largely on the type of draw, chip stacks, your read on your opponent, and other related factors.

Tip 38

Playing Drawing Hands in Tournaments

Here are some traps to avoid when on a draw in tournaments:

Paired Board

Don't draw to a straight or flush when the board is paired and the paired card is likely to have hit an opponent. A good example of this is a flop of J-J-10 when you hold K-Q. Yes, eight cards complete your straight, but there are no guarantees that your hand is live. Combinations such as A-J or J-10 can easily be out, so you may complete your straight and still lose the pot.

Overpaying When Heads Up

Don't overpay when heads up. If an opponent charges you a high price to draw to a straight or flush, this hurts your implied odds, and you should be inclined to fold. For example, if the pot contains $200 and your opponent bets $400, you aren't getting the correct price to draw to a straight or flush.

Your Hand

Board

Overplaying Against Dangerous Boards

Don't overplay sets or two pair on dangerous boards. Although these holdings are commonly considered to be made hands rather than draws, it is sometimes apparent on the turn that you are currently trailing to a straight or flush. You will need to improve to win; thus, your made hand is now technically a draw. Depending on the size of your opponent's bet, you might have to fold. Don't go broke with a set against an obvious made hand, and leave muttering to yourself, "I had a set. There was nothing I could do." There is—fold, unless the price is right!

Adding Value to a Flush Draw

When you hold a flush draw, there are nine cards that complete your hand. However, sometimes it won't take a flush to win the pot. If you also have two overcards to the flop, you may be able to make a pair and win, for a total of 15 outs. This possibility makes your hand the favorite to win the pot over a small pair on the flop.

One Mistake Not to Make

This hand was observed at the opening $2,000 no-limit hold'em event of the 2004 World Series of Poker. With $25/$25 blinds, player A raised to $50 and was called by player B (who had K♣ Q♣). Both blinds folded.

The flop came 10-9-5 with two clubs. Player A bet $50 and player B, understandably happy with the flop, raised to $100. Now, player

A moved all in for $1,900 more. Player B shrugged and folded his hand faceup, stating, "I like my draw, but I can't call that much."

Player B should have had his poker license revoked after this hand. His actions may well have cost him a big pot. Sitting in last position with a big draw, it is a huge mistake to give your opponent a chance to raise you off your hand. If it is bet to you, your best options are to either call or make a big enough raise that you are committed to the pot. A committing raise is fine, as you will either win the pot immediately most of the time, or will have a reasonable opportunity to win a big pot if called. A small raise such as the one made by Player B in the example is terrible; you probably won't get your opponent to fold, but you give him the opportunity to bet you out of the pot.

Player A   **Player B**

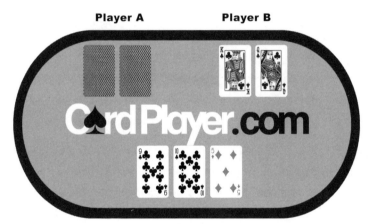

Board

Tip 39

Flopping a Set Or
Two Pair Against
an Overpair

As your hand reading skills improve, you will become better at identifying when an opponent is likely to be holding a big pair such as aces or kings. Since they are the best hands in the game, many of your opponents will become married to them; remaining that way even when things are clearly not working out. It is questionable whether A-A and K-K are even profitable hands in the clutches of certain eternal optimists early in the event.

It seems counterintuitive, but when you start with a small pair, you should actually hope that your opponent has A-A if he lets you see a flop for a reasonable price. Now, if you flop a set, you are poised to get all his chips. There is really no need to mess around and slow-play against a big pair, either. Your opponent probably won't expect you to make an oversized bet with a set, and you will likely get raised. The bottom line is that to realize all of the implied odds potential, try to play your hand in a manner that builds a big pot once you have flopped a set.

Tip 40

Some Comments on River Play

Riiver play can be tricky. Watch out for these situations:

Betting From Last Position

Be careful when betting for value from last position. While it is important to try to win as much as possible when you have the best hand, betting from last position in a no-limit game can be risky. The main problem arises when your hand is good, but not great. With a great hand, you are free to make a large wager, hoping to be called. However, when you hold a decent or good hand that is likely to be the best, you might want to extract some extra value by placing a small bet.

The danger here is that you will be faced with a tough decision should your opponent make a large check-raise. Although check-raises on the river are infrequent, they do happen, particularly if you have been leading at the pot the whole way and the board changes on the end. For example, suppose you hold A-K and the board shows K-9-3-7-8, with three suited cards. Your opponent has been checking and calling the whole way, with what appears to be either a worse pair or some kind of draw. Although betting the river for value is a desirable play in a limit game, it is very risky in no-limit, because your opponent just might choose to make a substantial check-raise. This obviously makes it very difficult for you to call with one pair. Overall, it is probably best to check the river in last position with just one pair, unless the board is very safe or your pair clearly appears to be the best hand and you put your opponent on a slightly worse hand that he can call a bet with.

Having some knowledge of your opponent can dramatically improve your ability to play correctly in this situation. Against weak calling station types, you can tend to bet for value frequently, as they won't check-raise on the river and might pay you off with many hands. When your opponent is a good, tricky player, you have to check more. For one thing, these players won't call with worse hands as often. And, they just might put a play on you, check-raising with a worse hand in an attempt to get you to fold your pair. The idea here is that the few extra chips you stand to win by getting called by a worse hand are not worth the risk of making the wrong decision if your opponent puts you to the test with a big check-raise.

Being Pot-Committed

If you have bet most of your remaining chips on the river, it appears as if you are committed to the pot. That is, your opponents

Your Hand

Board

feel that you will call should they raise you the rest of your stack. As a result, should you bet and get raised in this situation, your opponents will hardly ever be bluffing, and are actually welcoming a call. This means that you might be able to fold and save your few remaining chips if you don't have a big hand.

Some words of caution here are useful, though. First, if you decide to fold a legitimate hand to a raise on the end because you are certain you're beat, don't show it to the table. The last thing you want is for your opponents to think you make good laydowns. If they think this, they'll be firing frequent bluffs at you, forcing you to make many difficult decisions. Second, it is important to call if there are some hands you can legitimately beat. Your opponent might have raised to put you all in because it didn't cost him many more chips for a chance to bust you. He may not be sure his hand is the winner, but knows you can't hurt him much. So, if you feel you have even a fair chance of holding the best hand, you should call when you appear to be pot-committed.

Small Raises

Be wary of small raises on the end. When you make a $3,000 bet, and your opponent makes it $6,000 (and has more chips left), this nearly always represents strength. Your opponent is likely making a value raise here, feeling that you must call such a small raise but fearing you will fold if he raises more. Also, he is reopening the betting by making this small raise, giving you the chance to reraise. Most likely, this is what he wants. So, think twice before just tossing in the call.

Tip 41

How to Play in a Loose Game

Poker's dramatic growth in popularity has led to a high number of loose players who are new to the game. Whether you're playing a cash game with your friends or in an online tournament, chances are you'll often find yourself in a loose game. Here are some important guidelines for adjusting your strategy for success:

You'll Win Less Often, But Win More

Proper play will have you winning fewer hands but winning big when you do. The trick to winning against loose players is win a few big hands through a tight-aggressive style. Since there will be multiple players seeing almost every flop, only get involved when you've got strong cards.

Don't Bluff Much

There's no sense trying to bluff loose players, because they're more likely to call you down with weak cards. Bluffing will only lead you to lost pots and trouble.

Don't Slow-play Much

A common mistake is to assume that slow-playing is an effective strategy, but it's not. The reason is because loose players frequently chase draws with weak odds. To avoid watching your trips get ruined by an unlucky river card, bet aggressively to force out the drawing hands.

Thin the Competition

Do thin out competition with a medium hand even if one person may have a better hand. To win at a loose table, you cannot let too many players see the flop. If you choose to enter a pot with a medium-strength hand, narrow the field to one or two callers with a pre-flop raise. Be prepared to represent the flop even if nothing hits.

Thin the Field in a Tournament

Do thin out the field if antes and blinds are relatively high, as that is what you are fighting for. In late-stage tournament play, the antes and blinds will often constitute a large pot on each hand. Bet aggressively before the flop to narrow the field. If everyone folds, you've still won a decent number of chips.

Check Drawing Hands

Check when you are drawing to the nuts but can't stand a big raise. The implied odds when drawing to the nuts are very high, especially at a loose table. If you can't justify calling a large raise, simply check your draw. You won't need to worry about getting run down since you're the one on the big draw.

Tip 42

Learning Odds the Easy Way

You don't have to be great at math to learn how to calculate odds. This tip covers a quick shortcut you can use.

Let's say you just saw the flop and want to calculate the approximate chance you have of making your hand by the river. You can simply multiply your outs by 4 and you'll have the answer. The formula looks like this:

(Outs X 4) = % of getting a card you need

Remember, *outs* means the number of cards in the deck that will complete (or "make") your hand. For example, if you're holding 5-4 and the board reads 6-3-Q, a 2 or 7 will complete your straight. Since there are four twos and four sevens in the deck, you have eight outs. Eight multiplied by four equals 32. That means you have a 32% chance of making your hand in the next two cards. (The real percentage is 31.45%.)

This shortcut formula isn't perfect. If you have more than eight outs it slowly loses its accuracy. The actual percentage for nine outs is 34.97%, for 10 outs it's 38.39%, and for 11 outs it's 41.72%. (You may calculate your odds at www.CardPlayer.com.) But for situations in which you have between one and eight outs, you can calculate within about a half of one percentage point the chance of making your hand by the river simply by quadrupling your outs.

You'll gain a competitive edge over your opponents by implementing this powerfully simple technique.

Tip 43

Avoiding Tilt

Tilt is a dangerous condition in which a player behaves differently than normal, in a way that is based on emotion rather than logic. Tilt is often caused by bad beats or a huge loss. This condition is dangerous because it often leads to additional lost pots and, in a tournament, table elimination. Here follow some comments on tilt and how you can avoid it when playing no-limit hold'em:

Logic Not Emotion

Understand that poker is purely about logic, not emotion. All good poker decisions are based on logic and do not factor in emotion. The minute you begin making emotion-based assumptions or actions, you've lost control and your poker game will be left to outside forces.

Tilt Causes Aggression

Tilt usually makes you more aggressive. A player on tilt suddenly begins betting, raising, and bluffing more than normal. At first this may not negatively affect his game if he steals a few pots, but ultimately he'll take a stab at the wrong pot and suffer the consequences.

Your Brain is Playing Catch-Up

When you're on tilt, your brain is trying to catch up to previous chip counts. The reason tilt causes more aggressive play is because tilt is usually caused by a major loss. In poker, the general rule is that chip stack gains come slowly, and losses come quickly. It may take you four hours to rebuild a stack that loses 90 percent of its value in one pivotal hand.

Instead of accepting the new short stack size and adjusting accordingly, your brain has a tendency to try to catch up to its previous stack level as quickly as it fell. The mathematics don't work this way, though. It's easy to go from 1,000 chips to 100 chips quickly. But to go from 100 chips to 1,000 chips quickly is virtually impossible.

Separate Yourself

The most effective way to avoid tilt is to separate yourself from the game. You cannot necessarily combat tilt just by knowing what it is and why it happens. To truly overcome this condition, you must separate yourself from the game by sitting out a few hands, getting up from the table, or possibly moving to a different table. Do your best to avoid and overcome tilt and your bankroll will be much better off in the long run.

Tip 44

Some Advice About Stealing the Blinds

Stealing the blinds is a crucial strategy in no-limit hold'em. Especially when the cards aren't falling your way or you need to gain ground on an opponent, stealing blinds is often a quick path to success.

Big Risk, Little Gain

The biggest danger of stealing blinds is risking too much to win too little. You want to place a bet large enough to force your opponents to fold before the flop but small enough that you don't get burned if someone calls.

Have Some Outs When Stealing

Generally reserve blind stealing for hands that can hit something on the flop. You don't want to steal blinds with monster holecards, because then you've wasted great cards. But it's wise to steal blinds with cards that are reasonably playable if you get called. Blind stealing with hopeless cards is not a good idea. Suited connectors and small pocket pairs are great examples of blind-stealing hands. Since you'll usually miss on the flop, it's better to win before the flop. But if someone calls your preflop raise, you're still in a good position to take down the pot.

Position Is Everything

Since stealing the blinds largely depends on reading your opponents, it's almost a requirement that you have middle to late position when you attempt to buy the pot. Raising with a mediocre hand from an early position can lead to far more trouble than it's worth.

Look for Weakness in Opponents

You'll be able to spot weakness in your opponents quickly as the game progresses by watching their preflop betting habits. Some players liberally call the blinds but quickly fold to raises, some call almost any raise when in the big blind position because they feel invested in the pot, and some rarely ever make a call and instead stick to raising. Careful observation of each of your opponents helps you note these habits and more, thus paving the way for knowing when to make a steal.

Tip 45

Stealing Blinds in Tournaments

This tip discusses stealing blinds in tournament events, since tournaments have some nuances you should be aware of. Early in an event, defined as the pre-ante stage, the blinds are small. Although raising and picking up the blinds increases the size of your stack, this should not be your focal point. Yes, you need to steal some blinds to be successful in tournaments, but that comes later.

It is simply a matter of risk versus reward. To justify risking a portion of your stack, there must be some potential benefits. However, when the blinds are very small, you are laying an unfavorable price to try to win them. For example, with $10/$20 blinds and a stack size of $1,000, you risk somewhere in the neighborhood of $40 to $80 to win $30. Winning $30 several times isn't going to significantly help your chances of winning the tournament, but losing a few of these pots by getting your hand caught in the cookie jar will put a crimp in your plans.

Also, due to the cheap price and implied odds potential, you are generally more likely to get called early in the tournament. Later, the situation reverses itself: When antes are present, you stand to gain more by raising, plus play tends to tighten up. One more consideration on this topic is your table image. How you are perceived by your opponents is a determining factor in how they play marginal situations against you. You are generally better off later in the tournament that they are inclined to fold to your raises, as there is enough money in the pot that unless you hold a big hand, you don't mind winning uncontested. Too much early raising with inferior holdings hurts your credibility later on. Not only will you get called more frequently, but astute opponents will start coming over the top of you with hands that may not merit it, as they won't give you credit for a legitimate hand.

Tip 46

Folding Big Hands

As mentioned earlier, some of the most common hands players go broke with are high pocket pairs. This usually doesn't happen in a preflop all-in situation, either. What does happen is that you pick up pocket aces and raise, a few players call, and the flop comes. Then, one of your opponents is willing to get all the money in with you after the flop.

At this point, you need to consider a few things. First, you've already shown strength by raising before the flop, so your opponents likely are giving you credit for a good hand. Ask yourself: *Why does this player want to put all his chips in the pot when I've made it clear I have a good hand?* Chances are, he's improved his hand enough to beat a big pair. In a multiway situation in which you've raised preflop and then bet the flop, you must seriously consider folding if faced with a big bet or raise.

Good judgment is essential here. Some of your opponents are willing to go all in liberally with inferior hands, and if you are observant, you can learn who they are. Sometimes they have you beat, but you must usually call them. Your chances of holding the winner are too great to merit a fold against habitual bluffers.

Another consideration is the presence of draws. Some of your opponents play flush or straight draws very aggressively, so on a board such as 10-9-4 with two hearts, it is entirely possible your opponent is pushing a draw hand. The problem with this is that your overpair is only a modest favorite against a flush or open-ended straight draw, and is a big underdog if he flopped a set. If you add in the possibility of your opponent holding a hand like A-10, K-10, or J-J, you find that you sometimes must be willing to call a big bet here. Again, you need to use good judgment, taking into consideration your knowledge of your opponent.

When the board looks harmless (9-4-2 unsuited) and an opponent makes a big raise, warning bells should go off in your head. He isn't on a draw this time, so if you call, he will often show you a set. Once again, though, you can't automatically act in this situation. Think about factors such as how your opponent plays and his position in the hand. It is possible he is trying to protect a hand like 10-10 or J-J, so you must attempt to figure things out. There is no exact science here. Don't make a hasty decision, although your first inclination is likely to be correct. Study your opponent, and then act. You must possess the heart to make some big calls, but you also need to be capable of folding a big pair every now and then. You won't be perfect with these decisions, but nobody else is, either. The best players are right most of the time, though.

Tip 47

Making Probe Bets

Betting is the most important aspect of no-limit hold'em. If you generally choose to check and call, you'll never win at this game on a consistent basis. Betting is so crucial because it lets you know where you stand in the hand against your opponents. Without betting, it's extremely difficult to get a read on other players at the table, because you're giving them all the proactive decision-making power.

If you bet too many chips too frequently, however, you'll quickly find your chip stack diminished. So how do you balance these two opposing forces? The answer lies in probe bets, which are small bets designed to control the tempo of the game and learn about your opponents' hand strength.

A probe bet is generally 20 to 35 percent of the pot size. It puts your opponent to a decision to call, raise, or fold. If he calls, you can make educated guesses about his hand. He could likely be on a draw or have a low-to-middle pair, and is happy to see the next card on the cheap. If he raises, you're probably beat, and you know to lay down the hand if needed. And if he folds you've just taken down a pot without risking many chips.

The danger associated with probe bets happens most often against highly skilled players. Experienced hold'em opponents won't let you get away with probe bets very long without coming back over of the top of you whenever you make them. They'll stop respecting your bets and raises and your chip stack will begin to drain.

Use probe bets sparingly when it's up to you to open the betting and you're looking for more information about your opponents' hands. This can be a powerful technique when used properly.

Tip 48

Mounting a Comeback When Short-Stacked

Learning how to play a short stack is a vital skill when it comes to consistently beating no-limit hold'em tournaments. The number of times an experienced player has come back from the short stack and gone on to win an event is countless.

The reality is everyone falls victim to bad beats and tough luck. When it happens to you, use these tactics to grind your way back into the game.

Don't Wait Too Long

Don't wait too long before making a move. If your chips stack is approaching 10 times the big blind, it is time to make a move.

As the short stack, you do not have the luxury of waiting for premium cards before betting aggressively and taking stabs at pots. If you wait too long, even your all-in move will be ineffective and several opponents will join the pot just to bust you out. Make sure when you raise as the short stack that the amount is enough to narrow the field of callers or scare everyone into folding.

Choose the Right Conditions

Choose the right conditions to make your move. The cards you get dealt are only part of the equation. Pay close attention to which opponents enter any given pot and your position. These two criteria will help you choose the best opportunity to steal blinds or create a heads-up all-in situation to double upon.

If you get a strong hand that's probably ahead before the flop, push all your chips into the middle in hopes of getting one caller. If you're forced to make a move with mediocre holecards, do so from late position when a tight player is in the big blind, thus lowering the chances you'll get a call.

Move With Moderate Holdings

Make your move with pairs, two high cards, or even ace high. Depending on the table size and blinds, these hands are generally good enough to make your move. Remember, you either want to steal the blinds if they're significant enough to make a difference for your stack or double up against one opponent. Tripling up is rare, but certainly does occur.

After you've successfully stolen blinds or doubled up, don't just sit back and let your stack dwindle down again. Keep aggressively working on winning chips through calculated actions. With the right combination of luck and skill, you'll find yourself once again a serious contender in the event in no time.

Tip 49

Improving Your Position

A s discussed in the tips on position, the best place to be at the table is on the button. This tip explores how you artificially reap the benefits of the button without actually being there. This is achieved through a technique called "stealing the button."

The dealer position is powerful because it acts last after the flop. If you're sitting to the right of the button, or two seats to the right, you can often "steal" this power with a preflop raise.

For example, if no one has raised the pot preflop and you have playable cards, consider making a raise. Chances are the player on the button will fold to your raise unless he has something good. Since you're on his right, his doing so will now give you the leverage of the button position after the flop.

This is a fairly straightforward technique to be used sparingly. Use it too often and your opponents will quickly catch on. Great conditions for implementing this tactic are when you sense weakness at the table and want to set yourself up for taking down the pot either outright or after the flop.

An important part of this move is to know the opponents sitting to your left. Watch throughout the game how they behave from late positioning to learn their habits. Leverage this knowledge throughout a game or tournament to come out on top.

Tip 50

Practicing Good Waste Management Skills

Imagine you are playing at the final event of the World Series of Poker, with a $10,000 buy-in and $10,000 in starting chips. The blinds are $25/$50, and you are in the big blind. The action has been folded around to a man who says, "Raise." He then puts $3,000 into the pot. Huh? This player has just invested $3,000 to win $75. In the tournament world or anyplace else, this is not a very good risk-to-reward ratio. Perhaps this player was being tricky by overbetting two aces. However, when everyone has folded, he flashes J-J, while stating, "I always lose with this hand, so I didn't want any action." Well, he wasn't going to get any action unless his jacks were slaughtered. Think about it: Very few players would consider calling such a disproportionately oversized bet without a premium hand, probably aces or kings.

It is very important that you don't bet more than you need to accomplish your goals. In the case of the two jacks, this player could have won the pot with a much smaller bet. With $25/$50 blinds, even $500 is a big enough bet to eliminate all but the best hands.

By betting $500, he still stands to win $75, but can save $2,500 those times in which he runs into a bigger pair.

The same is true when you are bluffing. You want to bet an amount that is sufficient to make an opponent or two fold. However, there is a point beyond which all you are doing is burning up your own chips. For example, suppose there is $500 in the pot, and you have $1,500 left. On the river, all you have is a busted straight draw, and your opponent checks to you. You want to make a bet as a bluff, and a big enough one that your opponent will be hard-pressed to call. You could bet your whole stack, but is that really necessary? There is no point in risking $1,500 when a $500 bet is just as likely to work. With experience, you will become more adept at learning how much is enough in various situations. It is a balancing act between not betting enough (making it too easy for your opponent to call), and betting too much (costing you more than is necessary when you get called).

Sometimes you are holding what you either know or believe is the best hand, and you are faced with the decision of how much to bet. Obviously, if you have the nuts and know you will be called, then you can safely move all in. However, a huge bet is likely to scare off your opponents. On the other hand, a very small bet prevents your hand from realizing its value.

What you should do is find the most profitable bet size. You can use some math to help with this problem, along with an estimation of how likely your opponents are to call various sized bets. This chart is not from actual data, but is typical of the type of analysis that goes into determining what size bet is best:

Bet Size	Likelihood of Being Called	Return on Your Bet
$100	90%	$90
$300	75%	$225
$500	50%	$250
$1,000	20%	$200

As you can see, it is not necessarily in your best interest to bet an amount that virtually locks up a call. Rather, a larger bet may be more profitable, even if you don't get called as often. In this case, a bet of $500 has the best return, even though you won't be called as much as if you had bet less.

Tip 51

What to Do When You Get Moved to a New Table in a Tournament

As a tournament progresses and players are eliminated, tables are consolidated. If you survive for a while, at some point your table is likely to be broken and you will find yourself moved to a new seat. When this happens, you need to take stock of several factors at your new table.

First, you must observe how many chips each of your new opponents has. Stack size is of paramount importance in no-limit hold'em tournaments, and you simply *must* be aware of how each player at your table measures up. In particular, observe which players have either very large or very short stacks.

Players with a lot of chips can either bust or cripple you should you get involved in a major pot with them. If you have a big stack yourself, it is good to be aware of where the other big stacks are sitting, so that you can make better playing decisions. Stack size issues are covered in earlier tips.

Conversely, some of your new opponents may be extremely short-stacked. These players have to make a move soon, and often do so with an inferior hand, such as any ace or a small pair. If you are attentive to this when you arrive at a new table, you should have a better idea of the value of some of your hands. For example, when faced with an early-position raise from most players, hands like A-10 and A-J belong in the muck. However, if you see that the raiser is very short, he might be raising out of desperation rather than on the strength of his hand, so you may in fact have the best hand.

Another thing to observe when arriving at a new table is the body language and conversation of the other players. Spending five minutes observing your table often alerts you to players who may be on tilt; you can look for opportunities to play pots with them as they will tend to have weak hands.

Also, some players may send off signals that radiate either confidence or a sense of dejection.

Regarding the first type, you can probably assume that this player has been doing well, has a good mental state of mind, and is thus more likely to make good decisions. Confidence also aids players in making good raises and bluffs, so be on the lookout for strong plays from these players.

Other players seem dejected, perhaps due to some bad luck to this point in the tournament. Players sending these signals tend to expect bad things to happen to them. These are often the opponents you should be bluffing, unless they demonstrate that they will call down bets even when the situation looks grim.

While you are busy studying your new foes, you must be aware that they are sizing you up as well. If they are not previously familiar with you, the main piece of information they have on you is the size of your chip stack. You should realize that the size of your stack can have an impact on the way you are perceived psychologically by your opponents. For example, if it is early in the tournament and you have amassed a large stack by doubling up a few times, it is likely that you will be viewed as a loose, aggressive, and lucky player. Some opponents may fear you, while others may be more inclined to call your bets, feeling a player with this many chips must bluff a lot. If you can gain a sense of how each of your new opponents perceives you, you can use your big stack to your advantage.

If you arrive as a short stack, be aware that the other players will be gunning for you. You have nothing for them to fear—few chips to hurt them, plus it doesn't look like it's going to be your day. Your new opponents see buzzards flying around you if you come to the table as a short stack, and will be looking to finish you off.

Tip 52

When to Set Traps

Sometimes when you have a big hand, such as pocket aces, you want to play it aggressively throughout. Typically, playing a hand aggressively at every point is the best way to build a big pot. However, there are some situations in which you will lose your customers if you **play fast**, that is, betting aggressively. These are the times you should try to trap your opponents by playing your monster hand slowly. **Playing slowly** or **slow playing**, is to bet small, not show aggression.

Opportunities for trapping arise at various points in a hand. You may be dealt pocket aces and decide to just limp in with them before the flop, or just call a raise rather than reraise. Or, as the hand progresses, you might flop a big hand such as a full house or the nut flush, and opt to check or let your opponent do all the betting for a while. Basically, the main reason for playing your hand in this manner is that you feel you won't get any significant action if you play more aggressively. If you are likely to get action anyway, by all means play your big hand fast.

In some situations you don't want to trap, or slow-play your hand. One is when your opponent appears to be pot-committed, with most of his chips already in the center. Put him all in without delay, as he is unlikely to fold, and should you check, it is possible that a scare card such as the fourth of a suit will hit, causing him possibly to decide to fold and save his few remaining chips. Another time not to trap so much is against an excellent player. For one thing, this type of opponent is the most likely to see through your deception. And, if he can see what you are up to, you may find that you've become the "trappee" rather than the trapper, should he get lucky and draw out on you. So, play your hand fast against a top-notch opponent, and force him to make the tough decisions.

What types of situations and opponents is trapping most effective against? The ideal opponent is one who bluffs frequently, has a big stack, and tends to overbet the pot. Let's break that down a bit:

1. A player who bluffs frequently is likely to bet your hand for you, thus doing your job; however, should you bet your hand, he will likely fold.

2. An opponent with a big stack gives you the best opportunity to double up with your big hand. Thus, you should try to win a big pot, rather than simply try to win right away with a bet. By slowplaying, you might induce your opponent either to bluff off a significant portion of his stack, or make a strong second-best hand that he can ultimately call a big bet with.

3. An opponent who overbets the pot is likely to fire out a pot-sized wager or larger, either on a bluff or when he makes a decent hand (but one that's not as good as yours). So, slow-play your hand and give him the opportunity to do this. You don't need to put in an unsolicited big bet of your own if it will only cause him to fold, and he will very likely build your pot for you.

One more thing to add: You want to have a hand that is unlikely to be outdrawn for trapping to be a good strategy. Preflop, that means aces or kings. Later in the hand, that means a set (with a benign-looking board), nut flush (or close to it), or full house. You may want to slow-play a straight as well, but be careful doing this if a flush draw is present; you don't want an opponent to beat you for free.

Bonus Tip

Know Your Own Weak Tendencies

It is very important in no-limit hold'em to understand your own weak tendencies; that way you stay out of trouble. Similar to how every players falls into betting patterns and habits at the table, many of your lost pots can be traced back to the same few reasons.

Upon losing a pot, take mental note of the conditions at the table. What was your positioning? How many players saw the flop? Which opponent beat you? What were your starting holecards? When you begin noticing common themes among your losses, discipline yourself to get out of these situations before they start. For example, if marginal hands keep getting you in trouble after the flop, fold them before the flop next time.

If you're struggling to adjust your speed at the table, don't play as many hands. Take your time and focus only on what you can handle. If the same opponent keeps outplaying you after the flop, don't enter into a heads-up situation with him unless it's absolutely necessary.

Knowing your weak tendencies will help you fix leaks in your game by personalizing the strategies and techniques you've learned in this book. Ultimately, you'll become a much better poker player as you make these crucial adjustments.

Appendix

To succeed at hold'em, you should have a good working knowledge of odds and probability. Whether you do the computations in your head on the spot, or take some time to learn by rote the odds of making certain draws, you should not neglect this aspect of the game. The chart on the following page contains the chances for completing various draws in hold'em.

Notes on the Odds Chart:

- **# of Outs**—Total number of cards in the deck that will probably improve your hand enough to win.

- **Sample Situation**—The most common drawing situations for a given number of outs. This is not a comprehensive list; there are other potential draws.

- **After the Flop (2 cards to come)**—The chances of hitting one of your out cards either on the turn or the river, with only three cards on the board.

- **After the Turn (1 card to come)**—The chances of hitting one of your out cards on the river, with four cards already on the board.

- **Straight draw** means either an open-ended or double-gut-shot straight draw. (Both situations will complete a straight with two different cards.)

- **Flush draw** means that you already have four cards of the same suit, and need only one more. Completing a runner-runner flush draw (you have three flush cards and need two more) is much less likely.

- **Live overcards** means that you have one or two cards higher than anything on the board and you think making one of those higher pairs will be enough to win.

- If you'd like to calculate the chances of specific hand combinations among multiple players, there is a poker odds calculator available online at **www.CardPlayer.com**.

Post-Flop Drawing Chances (Approximate)

# of Outs	Sample Situation	After the Flop (2 cards to come)	After the Turn (1 card to come)
21	straight draw, flush draw, with two live overcards	70%	45%
20		68%	44%
19		65%	41%
18	straight draw, flush draw, with one live overcard	62%	39%
17		60%	37%
16		57%	35%
15	straight draw with a flush draw	54%	33%
14		51%	30%
13	flush draw with an inside (or gut-shot) straight draw	48%	28%
12	flush draw with one live overcard	45%	26%
11	straight draw with one live overcard	42%	24%
10		38%	22%
9	flush draw	35%	20%
8	straight draw	32%	17%
7		28%	15%
6	you have two live overcards, and need to make a pair	24%	13%
5	you have one pair, but need to hit your kicker for two pair or make three of a kind	20%	11%
4	inside (gut-shot) straight draw; also, you have two pair but need to make a full house	17%	9%
3	you have one pair, but need to hit your kicker for two pair	13%	7%
2	you have a pocket pair, but need to make a set (three of a kind)	8%	4%
1	you have three of a kind, but need to make four of a kind	4%	2%
7/10	you have three of a kind, but need to make a full house*	36%	22%

*The chances of making a full house (starting with three of a kind) are listed separately at the bottom because there are 7 outs on the flop, and 10 outs on the turn.

Glossary

active player: A player still in contention for a pot.

aggressive: Pertaining to a style of play characterized by much betting, raising, and reraising. This is not the same as *loose* play. Some of the best players are very selective about the cards they play, but when they do get into a pot, play those cards aggressively.

all in: Out of chips, due to having put one's remaining chips into the current pot while other active players still have more chips and have the option of further betting.

ante: One or more chips put into each pot by each player before the cards are dealt. An ante is not part of a player's next bet, as opposed to a *blind,* which usually is.

bad beat: The situation in which a strong hand is beaten by a long-shot or improbable hand.

bad beat story: A story told by someone who lost a pot, often a big one, in a *bad beat.* Usually no one but the teller is interested in hearing the story.

bet for value: Bet a hand with the intention of getting called by one or more lesser hands, as opposed to getting the others to fold. This usually implies betting a hand that has only a slight edge, and one that a conservative player would likely check with. Also called *value bet.*

bet on the come: Make a bet on a drawing hand, that is, when holding four cards to a flush or straight.

big blind: The player two positions to the left of the button puts chips into the pot equal to size of the limit of the game. Those chips (and the player who puts the chips in) are called the *big blind.*

big slick: A-K as one's holecards.

blank: A card, usually turn or river, that doesn't help your hand. This term also refers to a card that doesn't appear to help *anyone.* For example, if the board is K-Q-J-9 of mixed suits, a 2 on the river would be considered a blank.

blind: A bet put in by a player before he gets his cards. A *blind* is part of that player's bet if he comes into the pot, as opposed to an *ante,* which just "belongs to the pot." See also *small blind* and *big blind.*

blind thief: Someone who steals the blind, that is, opens a pot without having good cards, hoping the blinds will just throw their cards away and the opener can win the chips represented by the blind or blinds without having to actually play the hand.

break [a table]: When a table gets short-handed, particularly in a tournament, move the players to another table.

button: The disk or other marker that indicates the dealer position in a game dealt by a house dealer. Also known as *dealer button.*

call someone down: Check, and call all bets to the river.

calling station: A player who calls on the least pretext, often with hands that rarely win against legitimate bets. A calling station is someone who feels he just has to "keep you honest."

cap: The maximum number of raises in a round of betting.

chances: The likelihood of a particular event, usually expressed in the form of some kind of fraction or in the form of one number *out of* or *in* another. Compare with *odds,* in which the outcome is expressed as one number *to* another number.

chase: Try to catch a better hand with a worse holding.

check: Make no bet, but still hold your cards. You can check, and then call a later bet, fold when the action gets back to you, or raise.

check-raise: Check, often with a good hand, and then, when someone bets and it returns to you, raise.

coin-flip situation: A confrontation involving two hands in which the chances of each are relatively close to equal. The typical situation thus described would be a pair against two overcards, as, for example, A♦ Q♥ against 7♠ 7♥, with the pair being approximately a 55-45 favorite.

come over the top: Make a large raise or reraise.

community cards: The upcards dealt to the center of the table that are part of each player's hand.

complete hand: Five cards that constitute a straight or better. Also called *pat hand.*

counterfeited: Having a probable winner turned into a probable loser by the appearance on the board of another card of the same rank or suit as one of yours.

curiosity call: A call from someone who is positive he is beat but just wants to know what you had, often accompanied by a statement such as, "I knew you had me beat, but I just had to see it," or, "I knew you had me beat, but the pot was too big to fold."

dead money: Previous bets abandoned in the pot such that the players who made those bets, having folded, cannot win the pot. Dead money includes folded blinds.

dealer button: See *button.*

deep: Pertaining to how many chips a player has. Specifically, having a lot of chips.

discards: The players' thrown-away cards, sometimes together with the undealt cards that remain in the deck. Sometimes called *muck.*

dominated: The situation in hold'em of one hand being significantly ahead of the other, often because of having the same card in common plus a higher card. For example, K-Q offsuit is dominated by A-K offsuit. Also, any pair is dominated by any higher pair.

double gut-shot: A five-card combination with two "holes," such that any of eight cards can make it into a straight.

downcard: An unexposed part of a player's hand, delivered facedown by the dealer.

draw: An unmade hand.

drawing dead: Trying to make a hand that will lose if made. An example is drawing to a flush when an opponent already has a made full house.

drawing hand: Four cards to a straight or flush with cards to come, as opposed to a *complete hand.*

draw out: Beat someone's hand by drawing.

early position: The first few positions to the left of the dealer, or to the left of the blinds.

extra outs: Cards that improve a hand in more ways than the self-evident *outs.*

family pot: A pot with a lot of players, sometimes as many as all at the table.

fish: Easy-to-beat player, usually a *loose-passive* player.

flop: The three *community cards* turned faceup after the first round of betting.

free card: The situation in which there is no bet on a particular round, so players get extra cards without having had to risk additional money.

go all in: *Move all in.*

go in the tank: Sit and think, usually about an important decision, for an unusually long time.

gut-shot: The card that makes an *inside straight,* or, more commonly, the making of a straight by catching a card *inside.*

hold'em: A form of poker with two cards dealt facedown to each player, and five community cards dealt faceup in the center of the table.

holecard: Any one of the *downcards.*

house: A cardroom or casino, or the management of a cardroom or casino; often preceded by *the.*

human card rack: Someone who gets a lot of good hands.

implied odds: The ratio of what you should win (including money likely to be bet in subsequent rounds) on a particular hand to what the current bet costs.

kicker: The unpaired card (side card) that goes with a player's pair or set. For example, a player with A-K and a board of K-9-2 has a pair of kings with an ace kicker (something known as *top pair, top kicker*).

kicker trouble: Having an inferior kicker (side card) to a likely better kicker held by another player. For example, if you have A-2 and an ace appears on the board, if there is any betting, there is a good chance that at least one opponent has an ace with a better kicker.

late position: Positions to the right of the dealer, that is, those that make their decisions after the first few players have acted.

leave money on the table: Fail to extract as much as possible (by not betting with what is almost certainly the best hand).

limp: Open for the limit in a *structured limit* game, as opposed to coming in for a raise.

live one: A very loose player, usually implying one who loses.

loose: Having relaxed playing standards (and consequently playing more hands than other players); opposite of *tight.*

loose-aggressive: See *maniac.*

loose-passive: A *loose* player who plays passively. A loose-passive player is often termed a calling station.

maniac: Someone who bets and raises wildly and at every possible opportunity—with little correlation to the value of his cards. Also known as a *loose-aggressive player.*

middle pair: The situation in which a player pairs one of his holecards with something other than the highest card on the board.

middle position: Somewhere between early position and late position.

miracle: When poker players use this word, they generally mean the catching of a long shot, as, say, an inside straight or a third deuce when the player holds 2-2 against a higher pair.

move: [A] play. "In no-limit hold'em, going all in is a very powerful and important move."

move all in: Bet all your chips. Also, *go all in.*

muck: The *discards.* To throw cards into the muck means to discard them.

nut: The best possible hand for the situation. Thus a *nut* flush is the best possible flush that can be made. With four hearts on the board, for example, whoever holds the A♥ has the nut flush. Similarly, with a board of 6♥ 7♦ 8♦ Q♥ A♣, anyone with holecards 10-9 of any suits would have the *nut straight.* That hand would also be known as *the nuts,* because it is the best possible hand that can be made with that board.

nuts: See *the nuts.*

odds: The likelihood or unlikelihood of a particular event, usually expressed in the form of one number to a number.

offsuit: Descriptive of the holecards being of different suits, as opposed to *suited.*

one gap: Describing starting cards in which the two cards are two apart in rank.

on the button: In the *button* position.

on tilt: Playing badly. See *tilt.*

option: When the action is on the player who put in the *big blind,* and the pot has been opened for the minimum (that is, there has been no raise), that player may, if he wishes, raise. A house dealer may say "Your option," as a reminder.

outkicked: Losing with a pair because an opponent has the same pair, but with a higher kicker (side card). For example, you have J-10 and the board is J-9-6-3-2. If you lose to a player with A-J, you have been *outkicked.*

outs: Cards that improve a hand, usually used with reference to a hand that is not currently the best hand.

overcard: A card on the board higher than the rank of your pair.

overcards: Cards higher than your pair, or cards higher than any on the board.

overlay: Receiving a better return than the pot odds indicate. For example, if the odds against making your hand are 2-to-1 and the pot offers 9-to-1, your hand is an overlay.

overpair: A player's pair higher than any card among the community cards.

passive: Playing nonaggressively, that is, rarely originating bets and tending generally to call and not raise. Opposite of *aggressive.*

pat hand: Complete, or five-card, hand, that is, a straight or better.

play fast: Bet aggressively; make large bets.

pocket pair: A pair as one's first two cards.

position: Where a player sits in relation to the dealer.

pot-committed: Having put so much money into a pot that one feels obligated to play the pot to the end, perhaps by calling any subsequent bet.

pot odds: The ratio of the size of the pot compared to the size of the bet a player must call to continue in the hand.

put someone on a hand: Decide that a player has a specific hand. See *read a hand.*

rag: A card in the flop that probably doesn't help players who started with good cards.

rainbow: Of all different suits.

rake: Take a percentage of the pot, usually by the *house* as its means of making money on the game.

ram and jam: Bet and raise frequently and aggressively. Also, *play* fast.

read a hand: Make a conclusion about another player's holdings based on that player's actions, remarks, betting patterns, etc., and on the constitution of the board with relation to the preceding.

river: The fifth and final community card.

rock: An extremely tight player, one who takes few chances.

runner-runner: Flush or straight cards that arrive on the fourth and fifth cards, appearing for someone who, on the flop, had only three to that particular hand.

scare card: A scary-looking card for the situation. When two of one suit are on the board, the appearance of a third card of that suit may be a scare card for anyone for whom that card does not make a flush. If you had two pair when there were three spades on the board, you might worry about someone having the needed two spades with which to make the flush. And if the third of a suit is a scare card, the fourth suited card is even more so.

second pair: Forming a pair that consists of one of your holecards matching the second-highest card on the board.

semibluff: A bet made on a hand that is probably not the best at the time of the bet, but that has two ways to win: either by getting everyone else to fold or, if called, that might improve on succeeding cards.

set: Three of a kind. To *flop a set* means that (most often) one started with a pair and one of those cards was among the flop.

showdown: The point in a hand, after all the betting is over, at which the players turn their cards faceup for comparison with all active hands, to determine which hand wins the pot.

side pot: An auxiliary pot generated when one or more players run out of chips, and which those who ran out cannot win.

slow-play: Opting to not bet or raise with a good hand in the hope of trapping other players on this or subsequent rounds.

small blind: The player to the immediate left of the button puts chips into the pot equal to half the size of the lower limit of the game. Those chips (and the player who puts the chips in) are called the *small blind.*

smooth call: Call, and specifically not raise, on your turn.

solid: Conservative, not likely to get out of line; said of someone's play or a player.

steal position: In a game with blinds, a late position, often the *cutoff* (position one to the right of the button) or button; so used because it is most likely from this position that a player attempts to steal the blinds, that is, open with a raise in the hope of not getting called by either blind.

structured limit: Describing the betting structure of a limit game (as opposed to no-limit), that is, with bets at one level before and on the flop, and twice that level on the turn and river, such as $15/$30 hold'em.

suited: Descriptive of the first two cards being of the same suit, as opposed to *offsuit*.

tell: A mannerism that gives away your holdings.

Texas hold'em: The "official" name for hold'em.

the nuts: The best possible hand at a given point in a pot. See *nut*.

third pair: Forming a pair that consists of one of your holecards matching the third-highest card on the board.

tight: Playing very conservatively; showing little gamble; not likely to take a chance; having stringent playing requirements.

tilt: The state of playing poorly and irrationally due to emotional upset, often caused by the player in question having had a good hand beat by a freak draw from another player or the player having lost a pot because of his own bad play.

top pair: The situation in which a player pairs one of his holecards with the highest card on the board.

turn: The fourth card dealt to the center. Also known as *fourth street*.

underpair: A player's pair lower than any card among the community cards.

x: Shorthand for any unspecified card. A-x, for example, means an ace plus any other card. A-x suited is an ace plus any other card of the same suit.

Some of the definitions in this glossary have been adapted from *The Official Dictionary of Poker* (©2005 Michael Wiesenberg) and are used with permission.